THE
SPIRITUAL
BREAKTHROUGH
BOOK

Published by:
54TH STREET PUBLISHING
Savannah, Georgia. United States of America

THE SPIRITUAL BREAKTHROUGH BOOK:
Teachings, Prayers and Strategies to Guide You to Victory
by Elizabeth Ruggles Woods

www.spiritualbreakthroughbook.com

ISBN–13: 978–0692718216
ISBN–10: 0692718214

Cover design by: Shay Charles Awogbile
Book design by: Shay Charles Awogbile
www.shaycharles.com

THE SPIRITUAL BREAKTHROUGH BOOK

*Teachings, Prayers and Strategies
to Guide You to Victory*

Elizabeth Ruggles Woods

Illustrated by Shay Charles Awogbile

54th STREET PUBLISHING

This book is dedicated to the many brothers and sisters,
sons and daughters who make up the
Mission Teens family.

For the past eleven years, it has been my privilege to walk
a few steps with you as you journey into more of Jesus.

CONTENTS

1. IDENTITY

2. STRONGHOLDS

3. GOING FORWARD

ACKNOWLEDGEMENTS

I owe a debt of gratitude to many for help and encouragement in the process of writing this book. My husband, Tim, and my sons William and Walter have been my number one fans and stalwart encouragers for as long as they have been in my life. I am a blessed person to have such a family. They are all amazingly creative men and their advice has been incredibly valuable to me as I learned to navigate the waters of the creative process this first time.

My church family—the 54th Street House Church—has provided proof reading, concept testing, cheerleading, patience and love without measure throughout the entire process. Sandy Greenwaide, my number one fan, the communications director of 54th Street House Church, personal shopper, and partner in crime deserves special mention as does Shay Awogbile, the illustrator, cover designer, and all around project brainiac. Without these two this book would never have been written. Thank you both!

Several people have read early drafts and provided valuable feedback. Thank you to Laureen Burke, Taneiki Smokes, Gretchen Perez, Carol Reiterman and Greg Ruggles. You each have busy lives and your gift to me of time and encouragement is a treasure.

My final copy editor, Melissa Fletcher, is nothing short of a godsend. At a time when I needed a fresh set of eyes to help me get the last draft finished, God sent Melissa. Thank you, Michelle Womack, for the idea!

Early in the process, I received the benefit of some helpful feedback from Marios Ellinas who is himself a prolific writer. Thank you, Marios, for your words of advice and encouragement. I hope someday to be as disciplined a writer as you.

Finally, to my many friends and encouragers at Mission Teens, especially Julie Aspensen, Sabina Brackin, Abby Lishman and Jennifer Jones, thank you for the prayer support, the laughter and the love. You are so dear to my heart. The last five years has changed my life. It is my earnest hope that the contents of this book bless you on your journey.

FOREWORD

Don't give up!

If you are reading this book, you probably have your own ideas about spiritual breakthrough. Maybe you are frustrated with your spiritual life as it is. Perhaps there is a stubborn sin or character flaw which is defeating you and, although you have tried everything, you remain stuck. Perhaps you just know that there is more and you are hungry to go deeper.

Spiritual breakthrough is like overcoming writer's block or breaking a plateau when dieting or setting a new record in any endeavor. You need ideas. You need a new way of looking at things. You need coaching. That's what this book is all about.

This is a book about Christian spirituality but it is not a book about the status quo. Prepare to be challenged, even offended. Prepare to be pushed out of your comfort zone. This is not a book for victims or the passive. If you are ready to grow up and begin operating with spiritual maturity, this book is for you.

Spiritual breakthrough is available. You can break through to the next level of authority and freedom. The key is in your level of desire. What do you really want? Do you hunger and thirst for more of Jesus? He will give you what you truly desire. All you have to do is ask!

Just remember the first rule of spiritual growth: **first, it is difficult; then it is impossible; then it is finished.**

The key is perseverance. As Misty Edwards sings, "If you don't quit, you win!"

INTRODUCTION

This is a book for your spirit. Its purpose is to feed your spirit, to strengthen you so that you can grow into a mature son or daughter in the kingdom of God.

Most of what we read is intended to be consumed by our minds. We are familiar with this type of learning. We take in information and automatically connect it to prior knowledge. This process helps us to organize and make sense of new information. If we do this well, we can retrieve the data from our memories. When we encounter new data, we compare and contrast it to what we already know so that we can more fully understand. Our minds are wonderfully efficient at processing, cataloging and analyzing information so that we can interpret our experiences.

But how does our spirit learn? The spirit is designed to bear witness to truth. Therefore, our spirit learns by revelation and confirms the knowledge by the "witness" of the spirit. When you encounter something supernatural, your mind will try to process it, but if the encounter proves to be beyond explanation, another sort of learning becomes relevant. You will hear people say, "I can't explain this to you, but I know it's true." This is the best description of what we refer to as the "witness" of the spirit. It describes a "knowing" that is beyond our understanding.

As we study and learn and develop our mental capacities as followers of Jesus, we often neglect the development of our spirit and sometimes dismiss the practices required for our spirit to mature. We think that these are "mystical" practices and therefore based on superstition or possibly occult activity.

We are even offended by the suggestion that knowing "by the spirit" is real knowledge and we make a category for such experiences which declares them subjective and therefore useless.

With this much resistance, it is surprising that we have any spiritual experiences at all! It is the great gift of the Holy Spirit to grip our hearts with joy, hope, expectation, and even a little holy jealousy when we hear of encounters with the supernatural realm.

When you read this book, some ideas will offend your mind. I encourage you to notice and embrace that. Let your mind be a little offended; it will be good for your spiritual growth.

As you read and encounter a spiritual concept, let the Holy Spirit teach your spirit by revelation. Test the idea; does your spirit bear witness to the truth even if your mind cannot get on board yet? Let your mind take the lower place. If you learn to do this, you will open yourself up to an entirely new realm of the Spirit. Jesus said we must be like little children to receive the kingdom.

This is your invitation to grow smaller. Enjoy!

STRONGHOLDS AND COURTROOM INTERCESSION

The day we are born again is not only the day we are "saved" it is the day we begin our kingdom training. The goal of kingdom training is Christ-likeness. As we are transformed into the image of Jesus, we begin to think like Him, act like Him, love like Him. We become mature sons and daughters.

But how does all that work? Can we really expect to become like Jesus? What gets in the way of our training and how can we overcome every hindrance?

These are the questions we will answer together in this book. I believe you have in your hands powerful tools to accomplish the impossible. Father God wants you to become like Jesus. He is on your side and has committed amazing resources to ensure your victory. Let's learn together what those resources are and how to deploy them on our behalf.

Learning about strongholds and learning how to get free from them will be important keys for you. Read the chapter on strongholds carefully then read each chapter to see which, if any, applies to you.

You may have been thinking, "Oh, that's just me," but let the Holy Spirit teach you. Perhaps you will find that you have been thinking in a broken way which has hijacked your authority and used it to establish something untrue over your life!

You don't have to agree with every thought you have. Some of them are not true. You are more than you think you are! Let yourself believe it. That is not pride; it is humility. After all, you didn't do anything to earn the favor of God. It is a free gift from a loving Father.

Believing what the Lord says despite your own opinion is an act of faith.

As you practice recognizing strongholds in your thinking and learning how to take them down, your discernment will improve.

The first three steps to dealing with a stronghold—recognizing it, taking responsibility for it, and repenting of it—are complete as a strategy to tear down a stronghold in your mind (more detailed information is found in the chapter on strongholds). You may, however, feel as though a pattern of stronghold thinking (i.e. rejection, fear, bitterness) is found in your family line as well or even in your community. In that case, you have the option of taking it to heavenly court.

Courtroom intercession is one very effective tool in your spiritual weapons arsenal. Remember, the weapons of our warfare are spiritual and effective for the destruction of strongholds.[1]

Robert Henderson, David Herzog, and Ian Clayton have all written books on the courts of heaven which are excellent resources if you would like more information than I will include in this brief introduction. Also, Doug Addison of In Light Connection has begun online training workshops on the courts of heaven which are easily found at Doug Addison.com.

Here, I am limiting myself to explaining the role of the heavenly courts as we learn to take responsibility for our own thinking and then to use our authority to intercede in the courts of heaven for those around us.

To get an idea of prayer as a courtroom procedure, consider the story Jesus tells about a widow seeking justice from a judge:

> *"Now He was telling them a parable to show that at all times they ought to pray and not to lose heart, saying, "In a certain city there was a judge who did not fear God and did not respect man.*

---

1 2 Corinthians 10:3-5

There was a widow in that city, and she kept coming to him, saying, 'Give me legal protection from my opponent.'

For a while he was unwilling; but afterward he said to himself, 'Even though I do not fear God nor respect man, yet because this widow bothers me, I will give her legal protection, otherwise by continually coming she will wear me out.'"

And the Lord said, "Hear what the unrighteous judge said; now, will not God bring about justice for His elect who cry to Him day and night, and will He delay long over them? I tell you that He will bring about justice for them quickly. However, when the Son of Man comes, will He find faith on the earth?" [Luke 18:1-8]

Operating in the courts of heaven is an intercessory practice. It is a way to pray like the widow in Luke 18. It does not nullify the cross. It is also not a substitute for the work of the cross. We know that all sin is redeemed through the blood of Jesus. Without the blood, there is no remission of sins.

Repentance is completed not when we recognize sin or even when we feel bad about sin; it is finished when we receive and apply the blood of Christ to the sin.

Courtroom intercession is simply asking the Father to judge specific sin and injustice while we personally stand under the Mercy Covenant—the blood of Jesus. This we can do for ourselves and also as intercessors for others.

"Search me, O God, and know my heart; Try me and know my anxious thoughts; and see if there is any hurtful way in me, and lead me in the everlasting way." [Psalm 139:23-24]

We examine our own hearts first; then we accept responsibility for any sin we see there—any "hurtful way"—which refers to our broken thinking, too. The Hebrew is `otseb, which means "pain" and also "idol". We ask the Holy Spirit to find our defective thinking and lead us into another way.

We approach the throne of judgment with humility. As we come into His presence, we ask for judgment and justice just as the widow asked. She was seeking justice from an unrighteous judge but, as Jesus points out, we have a righteous judge who will bring about justice quickly. He has given us the blood of Jesus—a covenant of mercy—so that we can ask for His judgment without fear.

At the end of each stronghold chapter, there is an example of courtroom intercession as applied to each of the strongholds.

The idea is not to learn to recite the words exactly but to learn the protocol. We also have to remember that everything in the kingdom is a matter of intimacy. You cannot move forward without relationship. Apart from Jesus, we can do nothing. But we can do all things through Christ and in His strength.[2]

---

2 Philippians 4:13

1. IDENTITY

THE KAINOS OF GOD

MY DESTINY SCROLL: WHO AM I?

THE KAINOS OF GOD

Have you ever heard someone use this phrase? "After all, I'm only human!"

It seems true to us and it may even be a comfort when we keep messing up but the Bible doesn't say we are merely human. In fact, Paul uses this language as a rebuke to the church. "When there is jealousy and strife among you… are you not walking like 'mere men'?"[3]

The Scriptures teach that, "if anyone is in Christ he is a new creation."[4] The Greek word is kainos (kī′-nōs) which means something that has never before been seen on the earth. We are the kainos of God—a new creation, something brand new that has never before been seen on the earth.

---

3   1 Corinthians 3:3
4   2 Corinthians 5:17

If we are being honest, we have to admit that the body of Christ does not look like the kainos of God. We look like any other club or organization. Some of us have a better track record than others but we all look about the same to the world around us.

What has gone wrong? The problem is in our thinking. We are thinking like "mere men". Our expectations are too low. We have believed subtle lies about our identity and our limitations— lies we have been taught from our earliest recollection.

We believe what we are taught because we don't recognize that they are lies. Then we teach the same things to the next generation. It isn't intentional. No one is trying to get it wrong. These are diabolical lies, cleverly crafted with enough truth in them to make them seem reasonable. The lies make us comfortable when we disappoint ourselves and each other.

These lies are organized into what are called 'strongholds' in the New Testament [2 Cor. 10:3-5]. Their purpose is to keep us from the knowledge of God (we'll talk more about that later). Some examples are rejection, fear, bitterness and accusation. We believe no one loves us or God could never forgive us or we can never forgive ourselves. We worry about the future, the past, our family and friends—all the while considering ourselves normal Christians.

One of the reasons we need a community of believers is to challenge the things we believe. Unfortunately, communities of believers often impose uniformity in the name of unity. People are uncomfortable with variety and differences. Out of fear and insecurity or ignorance, we accept the standard that everyone else is accepting and we abandon our daily pursuit of intimacy with Jesus.

Our Christian life is meant to be lived in communion with our shepherd, having conversations about ourselves, others and all of creation—learning how to understand mysteries and how to know his voice. Instead, we follow other Christians—either fearing to change any of our traditions or so addicted to change that we chase one fad after another—the sheep following the sheep in circles.

We don't do this on purpose. We really do want more. It's just that we have convinced ourselves that this is the best we can hope for until we die. Then every tear will be wiped away and all of this mess will be fixed.

More and more believers are awakening to the presence of a problem in our thinking. Many are still too nervous to consider the real implications of this problem, but it is a simple one to define. Will we continue to walk according to our own understanding—according to our religious flesh? Or will we repent of this folly and begin to follow the Holy Spirit?

If we choose to follow the Holy Spirit, we choose to abandon our independence. We acknowledge our dependence on Him and our utter lack of ability to change ourselves. We abandon religious thinking in order to embrace our identity as those who are completely loved and wanted by our Father in heaven. We accept our place as a son/daughter and we say yes to the process of becoming one with Christ.

> *"Or do you not know that your body is a temple of the Holy Spirit who is in you, whom you have from God, and that you are not your own? For you have been bought with a price therefore glorify God in your body."*
> *[1 Corinthians 6:19-20]*

Glorify God in your body. Be the temple of the Holy Spirit. Expel every bit of the darkness that still speaks to your mind from the wounds of your past. Believe everything the Father is telling you about who you really are.

CHANGING OUR MINDS

The word "repent" in the New Testament is translated from the Greek μετανοέω, "metanoéō."[5] It means to change one's mind for better; to think differently or to reconsider (morally, feel compunction).

In other words, to repent is to reconsider and change your mind about something in such a way that afterward, you sustain your new mindset and forsake your old way of thinking.

Repentance is a sustained change in our thinking which will result in changed behavior.

The battle begins in our mind. It is a battle for control. When we choose to live in our truest identity, for example, we bring our mind under the authority of our spirit. In order to break through to a new level in Christ, the first thing we must consider is how we think.

Although the scriptures exhort us to live by the Spirit,[6] most of us have learned how to live according to our flesh rather than according to the spirit. If you were raised in church you were probably taught that "flesh" equals sin. Therefore, not living according to your flesh simply means trying to avoid sin. But what are the mindsets over which we need to repent?

I propose to you that any mindset which contributes to insecurity or inferiority needs our repentance. We must agree with the Holy Spirit and break agreement with every lying spirit.

Living by the Spirit does not mean that we work hard to avoid sin. In fact, trying merely to change your behavior in order to avoid

---

5 Strong's Concordance <u>G3326</u> and <u>G3539</u>
6 Romans 8:1–19

living according to your flesh is to approach the matter from an entirely useless perspective. This is the perspective of our natural mind (earthly wisdom); the scriptures counsel us against relying on our own understanding in matters of the Spirit.[7]

Romans 8:1–19 goes beyond simply condemning the life lived according to the flesh. Paul says we must die [v.13] if we are living by the flesh. There is no middle ground between the life lived by the Spirit and the life lived by the flesh. They are at odds. One leads to life; the other to death. If we live by the Spirit instead of by the flesh we will grow up in all ways. We put aside childish things and become adults in the Spirit as part of our normal maturing process.[8]

It is our spirit taking his/her proper place that really makes a difference. The spirit of man is meant to rule and reign—first, over our soul and our body and then over our kingdom responsibilities. Our job is to submit; that is all. Paul asks in Galatians if it is possible to begin by the Spirit and end up in the flesh. He is trying to point out that we cannot accomplish the goal of submitting to the Spirit by doing things to justify ourselves.

This is His plan. "For those whom He foreknew, He also predestined to become conformed to the image of His Son, so that He would be the firstborn among many brethren."[9] He is the firstborn; we are the brethren!

---

7 Proverbs 3:5–6
8 1 Cor. 13:11
9 Romans 8:29

My Destiny Scroll:

WHO AM I?

"I will give thanks to You,
for I am fearfully and wonderfully made;
Wonderful are Your works,
And my soul knows it very well.
My frame was not hidden from You,
When I was made in secret,
And skillfully wrought in the depths of the earth;
Your eyes have seen my unformed substance;
And in Your book were all written
The days that were ordained for me,
When as yet there was not one of them."

[Psalms 139: 14–16]

Let's begin with a concept that is rooted in rabbinical tradition. I offer it here because it is likely that Jesus was taught this world view. It is consistent with the testimony of the Scriptures and the character of God the Father.

The rabbis teach (based partly on Psalms 139:16) that "all souls were created at the beginning of time, and are stored in a celestial treasury until the time of birth."[10]

Before you were born, they teach, you counseled with Father God and together you agreed to your assignment in the earth. The Lord God wrote upon your heart certain things about your identity and your purpose (your destiny scroll) and recorded everything in your book. The rabbis teach that we all fall into forgetfulness as we pass from heaven to earth but babies and children retain memories of heaven and have the ability to see angels better than adults.

The goal of life, then, is to recapture your childlike faith. It is not to "find yourself" but to remember who you are! Your life's journey is to find again what is written on the destiny scroll of your heart. It is to accept the truth about who you are and who you always were.

If you choose to believe this, your views of life, circumstances, pain, destiny and identity will be radically changed. There are no victims in a universe where we all asked to be born and volunteered to come to this troubled planet in order to spread the kingdom of love to every corner of existence.

Perhaps giving credence to an ancient mystical idea is too much of a stretch for you. Consider the clear implications of the following scriptural passages. The New Testament clearly indicates a plan for

---

10 Rabbi Aryeh Kaplan, "The Soul". From <u>The Handbook of Jewish Thought</u>, (Vol. 2, Maznaim Publishing.

us as sons and daughters of a loving heavenly father—a plan that has been in place since before the foundation of the world!

- He blessed us with every spiritual blessing in the heavenly places. [Eph. 1:3]
- He chose us in Jesus before the foundation of the world. [Eph. 1:4]
- He predestined us to adoption as sons. [Eph. 1:5]
- We have an inheritance and were predestined for His purpose. [Eph. 1:11]
- We were created for good works which God prepared beforehand for us to walk in them. [Eph. 2:10]
- He predestined us to become conformed to the image of Jesus. [Rom. 8:29]
- He called those whom He predestined. [Rom. 8:30]

"I pray that the eyes of your heart may be enlightened, so that you will know what is the hope of His calling, what are the riches of the glory of His inheritance in the saints, and what is the surpassing greatness of His power toward us who believe. These are in accordance with the working of the strength of His might which He brought about in Christ, when He raised Him from the dead and seated Him at His right hand in the heavenly places, far above all rule and authority and power and dominion, and every name that is named, not only in this age but also in the one to come. And He put all things in subjection under His feet, and gave Him as head over all things to the church, which is His body, the fullness of Him who fills all in all." [Eph. 1:18-23]

In the Old Testament, Psalm 139 makes a strong statement that Yahweh knew us before we were even conceived and Jeremiah was told by the Lord that before he was formed in the womb, the Father knew him and consecrated him to be a prophet to the nations.[11]

---

11 Jer. 1:5

I invite you to ponder this concept for a moment. What if the life you have right now is the life you chose from before you were even conceived? Maybe you remember thinking as a child, "I didn't ask to be born!" What if that isn't true? What if you are an eternal being that is designed to find its origins in a loving God and to be restored to Him?

In one sense, when Jesus told the story of the prodigal son, He told this story. The son, loved by his father, strikes off into the unknown with his inheritance. There is no indication that the son intends to waste his life—only that he is excited about the adventure. He is foolish and indulgent and, in the process, he forgets who he is and what he was born to do.

After he has used his resources and his time poorly, he comes to himself (while considering the benefits of eating pig slop). He has abandoned all hope of being restored as a son but makes a plan to return to the house of his father asking only to be treated as one of the servants.

His father has never forgotten him. He has watched the road for a sign of his son's return almost since the day he left.

"But while he was still a long way off, his father saw him and felt compassion for him, and ran and embraced him and kissed him. And the son said to him, 'Father, I have sinned against heaven and in your sight; I am no longer worthy to be called your son.'

But the father said to his slaves, 'Quickly bring out the best robe and put it on him, and put a ring on his hand and sandals on his feet; and bring the fattened calf, kill it, and let us eat and celebrate; for this son of mine was dead and has come to life again; he was lost and has been found.' And they began to celebrate."

[Luke 15:20–24]

The parallels are interesting between the story of the prodigal and the story of mankind journeying from heaven to earth with a destiny scroll in his heart. The father gives his son an inheritance. The son is so focused on the present and trying to enjoy his life, he forgets who he is and wastes his inheritance. When he has no other choice, the son goes back to his father but shame compels him to ask for a lesser position in his father's house. When the father sees his son returning, he goes to him and restores everything to him.

The story of the prodigal is about the character and attitude of our heavenly father toward us. He forgives all because he knows we are his household— sons and daughters with inheritance. He wants us to come home to Him.

Too often, we seek only the place of the undeserving servant in our father's house. Our sense of insecurity and real shame inhibit the belief that our father wants to shower his love on us. What if he has a ring for your finger and a robe for your back? Could you accept such love? Or is the idea of such forgiveness too offensive for you?

The cross of Christ—the means by which we are forgiven and restored to our proper place in the household of God—is "foolishness" to those who are unable to accept it as our means of rescue.[12]

These scriptures testify to truths that are written on every believer's heart:

- I am a friend of God…James 2:23
- I am a carrier of the kingdom…2 Corinthians 5:20
- The evil one touches me not…Romans 8:31–39
- I bear the image of Jesus…2 Corinthians 3:18; Romans 8:29
- I am unique in creation...Psalm 139:16

---

12 1 Corinthians 1:18

Take a moment to ponder these few scriptural truths.

Once you acknowledge the basic truths written on your heart, you are invited to go further; you are invited to open your testimony scroll. In order to do so, you will need to:

- Acknowledge that you have a scroll and that you have the capacity to unroll the scroll.
- Activate faith; believe that God wrote things for you to do.
- Confess that you have not walked according to His desire; you have walked according to the record of your soul and body rather than your spirit.

That last one is a step of repentance. While we may have been ignorant of God's ways in this, we still repent because we are choosing a new way of thinking.

We will repent often throughout this book. Not because we are sin conscious and we are accused in everything but because we are God conscious and when we see our wrong thinking we want to come into agreement with the mind of Christ.[13]

As we come to terms with unhelpful thinking about our identity and God's heart towards us, we acknowledge our sin and bring it to the cross.

---

13 Romans 12:2; 1 Corinthians 2:16

PRAYER:

Father, today I exercise faith to believe that you have written a scroll, a testimony of the plans to which you and I agreed before I was conceived—plans about my life, things that I would do that no one else can. I acknowledge that I have lived according to the record of my body and soul and I repent of this and choose instead to live out of my spirit. I acknowledge that I am a supernatural spiritual being. I believe that I'm going to walk with you, Father, in the things that you have written.

Today, by faith, I open my heart up to your presence. I expose my heart to you and in my heart I unravel the testimony of the scroll that you wrote for me. I acknowledge before the supernatural world that I am a son of God (benim), born by your spirit. I am going to walk in a kingdom that will be displayed around me in signs and wonders. I'm going to be seen as benim, walk as benim, called benim, known in heaven as a friend of God.

Lord, today, as I open the testimony of my scroll, I ask that you read what you have written; that as you speak in heaven, you would release out of heaven your agreement that I will become on the face of the earth everything you have called me to be. I receive into my heart your voice that you are well pleased with me, that I am your child, that I have been called to be where you are; to be with you and in you.

Today, I seal inside of my spirit being, the testimony of the Son of God. I seal it by faith. I open my heart and display the kingdom to those who stand here. Let my heart bear your image and let it be revealed in the face of the earth. In the name of Yeshua, Amen![14]

---

14 This prayer is a prayer by Ian Clayton offered here with some minor edits

THE WORLD, THE FLESH, THE DEVIL

Once we begin to remember who we are, we still have opposition to overcome. We have enemies. An ancient version of the Catechism of the Catholic Church, a book of the doctrines of Catholic Christianity, clearly names our spiritual enemies. Fighting against us on our journey into our full identity in Christ are "the world, the flesh, and the devil."[15]

I like that the devil comes last on the list. We should acknowledge our 'ancient foe' without surrendering authority to him. The devil is not responsible for every evil under the sun. He may make an offer but we still have free will and our choice matters. Evil is made manifest in the world when we choose it. Without our choice to agree with the lies of the enemy, evil could not flourish.

I have a friend named Denny Strickland who lives in Heaven now with a growing number of my friends and family. He used to say that some of the hardest work a person can do is to accept responsibility for his or her part when things go wrong. I believe this is true. We can't grow up as spiritual sons and daughters until we accept responsibility for our own thinking and the behaviors that are holding us back.

It's true enough that other people will sometimes get in our way.

Relationships are complicated by insecurity, inferiority, envy, competition and fear. People will sometimes act in their own self-interest rather than support our attempts to grow.

---

15 A Dictionary of Biblical Tradition in English Literature, pp. 850-851. David L. Jeffrey. Wm. B. Eerdmans Publishing, 1992

It's also true that we have to deal with spiritual forces of wickedness in high places seeking to prevent us from inheriting our promises. And the culture itself—television, films, music, social media, etc. — is often toxic to kingdom values.

Still, the hardest work we will do is to address our own thinking. If you wonder if that's true, here are some new thoughts for you to try out:

- You have a destiny that was written long before you were born.
- God is not mad at you or disappointed in you.
- God is not waiting to punish you.
- Satan has no authority over you.
- Angels encamp around your life to help and protect you.
- As a follower of Jesus, you are a citizen of heaven now.
- As a son of God, heaven is open to you now.
- The same spirit that raised Jesus from the dead lives inside of you.
- You are something never before seen on the earth.
- We are not going to heaven; we are coming from heaven.

Are some of these ideas new to you? Uncomfortable? Hard to believe? They were hard for me to get my head around until the Holy Spirit revealed them to me as truth firmly supported in scripture.

We'll be discussing these ideas in later chapters but, for now, just notice which of these stretches you.

2. STRONGHOLDS

Strongholds:

DEFEATING STRONGHOLDS

"For though we live in the body, we do not wage war in an unspiritual way since the weapons of our warfare are not worldly, but are powerful through God for the demolition of strongholds. We demolish arguments and every high-minded thing that is raised up against the knowledge of God, taking every thought captive to obey Christ." [2 Corinthians 10:3–5]

A stronghold is a dysfunctional pattern of thinking that is held together by wrong conclusions about reality. The word 'stronghold' comes from the Greek ochuron, meaning 'to make firm; a prison'. A stronghold begins as a thought but if unchecked, it will manifest as sin.[16]

Wrong thoughts come in through our life experiences, especially unhealed trauma. They contain elements of our fallen nature and manifest as unbelief, fear, addictions, bitterness, envy, accusation, rejection, etc.

You can identify a stronghold by the following characteristics:

- It is a habit structure of thought.
- No conscious thought is required to think it; it is automatic.
- It is nearly unrecognizable to us as a lie.
- We feel protected by believing it.
- Our wrong thinking keeps us from hearing the truth.

Strongholds are rooted in lies which <u>seem true</u> but have their origin in another kingdom.[17]

"The devil...was a murderer from the beginning, and does not stand in the truth because there is no truth in him. Whenever he speaks a lie, he speaks from his own nature, for he is a liar and the father of lies." [John 8:44]

We tear down strongholds by establishing God's truth.

"For My thoughts are not your thoughts, nor are your ways My ways," declares the Lord. "For as the heavens are higher than the earth so are My ways higher than your ways and My thoughts than your thoughts." [Isaiah 55:8-9]

A thought cannot become a stronghold if you bring it into captivity!!!!

---

17   Concepts derived from "For Your Life" seminar by Pastor Henry Wright

TAKING RESPONSIBILITY

When I first began to resist stronghold thinking, I would practice the three R's in order to help my mind become renewed.

1. Recognize the thought
2. Take Responsibility for entertaining wrong thinking
3. Repent by tearing it down and bringing it under the blood

Amazingly, I was able to recognize lies for a long time without actually getting to repentance over them. Even now, if I'm going to get stuck, it is there between recognition and repentance in the place where I need to take responsibility.

For me, the problem with taking responsibility is often the presence of guilt and shame. I stand accused of a wrong and I must make a defense. All I can think of is "I am guilty—there is no defense. How could I have done this thing?" So you see my mistaken thinking.

"I am guilty, there is no defense" is honest but incomplete. I do not stand accused before God. Though I am guilty, the sacrifice has already been made for my sin. When He desires to correct me, the experience is more like, "Come let us reason together..." not, "Wretched sinner, how dare you transgress?"

My mistake is to confuse my accuser with the voice of the Holy Spirit! To the Lord, I owe immediate obedience; to the Accuser, I owe nothing.

My question, "How could I?" is rooted in pride. In an honest assessment of myself, I see that apart from the grace of God, I am capable of every evil under the sun. The greater surprise is that God could use me at all for His purposes. The truth is, He greatly desires that I mature in the things of the spirit so that I can be put to good use in the Kingdom.

"Look, that is rejection talking to me" or "I see a spirit of fear" is not yet victory but it is certainly the first step. When we are able to discern the battle, we are not far from victory! As soon as we recognize it, we are already halfway to taking responsibility for our agreement with it, for listening to the lie.

Once we say, "Yep. I let that lie talk to me. No one else did," then we are a mere breath away from repentance. "What was I thinking?" can easily become, "I break all agreement with that lie in the name of Jesus!" And the hatred of that lie becomes resistance to it.

See how easily we move from frustration to victory once we take responsibility! The fear of rejection had the power to keep me from taking responsibility until I got it into my spirit that He loves me, He's not disappointed in me and He will never leave me (Go back and read that sentence again slowly until you believe it).

The TRUTH had to answer the lie. And He did!

Deuteronomy 10:15; Isaiah 62:5; Psalms 139:14-15; 2 Cor. 5:17; Rev.21:9 Rom. 8: 30-39; Zech. 2:8; Eph. 1:3-8.

MATURITY

I'm going to suggest something uncomfortable to the body of Christ. Spiritual maturity is not achieved through the perfecting of your doctrine or theology. One is not a mature believer when answers to all the difficult questions fit into a perfectly functioning system of thought.

Maturity in the kingdom is measured the same way maturity in a family is measured: responsibility. We must take responsibility for our thoughts and for our actions, fully submitting them to examination and repentance. We will need to ask for help to see exactly where the cross needs to be applied.

Once we mature in the governing of our own soul, the Father wishes us to accept responsibility for things around us. We will be tried and tested in the stewardship of our time, talent and treasure. Each time we steward well, we will be trusted with more so we grow by degrees in responsibility.

But responsibility alone will not make us fully mature. The older brother in the story of the prodigal was responsible but he was not mature. He lacked the compassion and wisdom of his father. Maturity in the kingdom is responsibility plus Christlikeness.

The Greek word HUIOS in the New Testament is the word for mature son. The meaning connotes a degree of yieldedness. Jesus is HUIOS. He models this for us by explaining that, "The son can do nothing of Himself, unless it is something He sees the Father doing; for whatever the Father does, these things the Son also does in like manner."[18]

As sons and daughters (benim) of God we are meant to grow into maturity. When we are born "from above" into the kingdom of God we are like babies. The word used in the scriptures is nepios. It is one of the five Greek words that all mean 'son' but each indicates a different stage of maturity.

---

18 John 5:19

The nepios are untaught, unskilled, immature infants.[19] The next stage of maturity is the paidion.[20] This means 'little child or half grown' and corresponds roughly to a child between the ages of two and twelve. Next we have the teknon[21] —sort of like teenagers—then the huios[22] who are fully yielded and obedient sons, then the teleios[23] —fully mature spiritual adults.

God loves babies. Babies should act like babies. However, it is unnatural for babies to remain babies. Our spiritual lives should change as we grow. We ought to become more confident in our relationship with God the Father, Son and Spirit. We should know His voice and learn His ways. Our hearts ought to become like His heart as we learn to love what He loves. Eventually, we are meant to be trustworthy enough to accept responsibility for ourselves (read the book of Galatians) and our households and, finally, over kingdom government.

The gospel is an invitation to follow the King whose government has no end. If Jesus is the King of kings, then who are the kings? He made us a nation of kings and priests![24]

---

19 Gal. 4:1–3; 1 Cor. 3:1–4; Eph. 4:14–15; Heb. 5:13; Matt. 28:10; Matt. 11:25; Luke 10:21; Rom. 2:20
20 Prov. 13:24; Prov. 19:18; Prov. 22:15; 1 John 2:13,18; Heb. 10:25; Mark 10:15; Luke 2:40; Heb. 12:1–11

21 Acts 2:39; 3 John 4; Gen. 18:19; Ex. 12:26; Deut. 6:7; John 13:33–35; Num. 8:23–24; 2 Tim. 2:15
22 Matt. 3:16–17; Rom. 8:14–21; Gal. 5:22; 3:26; Eph. 5:19; 4:7–24; 1 Thess. 5:17–22; Rom. 12:1–2; 1 Cor. 2:9–13; John 16:12-15

23 1 John 4:18; Heb. 9:11; 5:14; James 1:4; 3:2; Eph. 4:13; Matt. 5:48; Col. 3:14; 4:12; Phil. 3:15; 1 Cor. 2:6;14:20

24 Revelations 5:10

As priests, we have authority to administer the sacrificial blood of Jesus. As kings, we have a governmental role. We are handed keys. Jesus turns to Peter and says, "Here are the keys. Everything you open will open; everything you shut will shut." [Matt. 16:19; John 20:23]

This is the binding and loosing passage. Whatever you bind on earth is bound in Heaven; whatever is loosed on earth is loosed in Heaven. Our word is meant in the earth to signify authority as in Heaven. But this can only happen if we mature and grow and become like our heavenly Father.

When Jesus was baptized in the Jordan, he was given authority like the Father's authority. The voice from heaven said, "This is my Son, my beloved Son; listen to Him."[25] This is an affirmation of Jesus' authority on earth—the exact same authority on earth that He carries in Heaven.

We tend to look at Jesus and say, "Jesus was special; he was the son of God. There is only one of him. I can't be anything like him. He was perfect. I'm not perfect. I'm no Jesus." But the plan God had in mind when he became incarnate and came into the earth as one of us was, in fact, to show us how to become like Him.

We are meant to be like Jesus. Seriously! And that should not conjure up images of a strange brand of alienating, irrelevant piety. Jesus was real—a down-to-earth sort of person that others liked. He still is that sort of person and He desires real relationship.

---

25 Mark 9:7; Matt 3:17

PRAYER FOR THE DESTRUCTION OF STRONGHOLDS:

Father, I **recognize** all mindsets of lack, limitation, restriction, constriction, scarcity, poverty mindsets, all rejection, all misunderstandings, all confusion, all fear, all addiction, all religious mindsets, as **enemy thinking** in my mind.

I take **responsibility** for agreeing with these lies.

In the name of Jesus, I now **break my agreement** with these lies and I cancel the covenants I have made with darkness. In Jesus' Name, I break the power of every stronghold within my mind and within my emotions. I surrender my will to your lordship, Jesus.

I apply the blood of Jesus to this sin and I wash my mind clean with the blood of the Lamb. I cleanse my entire soul with your blood. I command healing into my body and restoration of body, soul and spirit to their proper relationship to each other and in you. Father, based on the blood covenant of Jesus, remove the record of my sin from heaven, restore to me the joy of my salvation and renew a right spirit within me.

I am redeemed by the blood of the Lamb.

THE STRONGHOLD OF UNBELIEF

My friend, Timothy, has been hearing the voice of God since he was two years old. At four, his brother (who was six at the time) told him that Jesus wanted to live in his heart.

Puzzled, Timothy asked, "How can Jesus live in my heart? He is so big!"

"Tim," his brother replied with advanced theological insight, "He's God! He can do anything!"

With the simplicity of a child, Timothy accepted that answer asking, "Jesus, do you want to come live in my heart?"

Jesus said, "Yes, I do!" so Timothy invited him to come in.

From that point on, the voice that had been speaking into little

Timothy's ear began speaking from within his heart.

Tim is a grandfather now. When he tells this story, his eyes fill with tears at the thought that Jesus wanted to come live in his heart all those years ago. That He still speaks from within his heart and has never stopped speaking to him is a miracle of love that is beyond human understanding.

This is the gift of love offered to each of us. It is a level of intimacy with the king of the universe that makes no earthly sense; yet it is given to us for the asking.

How can this be? It's so simple: He's God! He can do anything!

In order to enter the kingdom, Jesus says, you must become like a little child. [Matthew 18:3]

*　　　*　　　*

There was a time when I read Mark 9:17–29, the story of the boy with a deaf and dumb spirit, and thought, "We have a medical explanation for that miracle now. Too bad those guys didn't seem to know what epilepsy was. They actually thought it was a demon!"

Does that line of reasoning sound familiar to you? It's pretty arrogant, though, to suggest that Jesus didn't know what he was talking about. After all, Jesus could have healed the child but he did not. He cast out a demon.

My mind has had to come to grips with the clear presentation of scripture. Demons exist and they do torment people. It's not all explainable by medical diagnoses or psychological descriptions.

We humans are a trinity—body, soul and spirit. Our mind and our emotions are part of our soul. Sometimes we will have a soul sickness; sometimes a bodily sickness and sometimes we will have a spiritual sickness. To accept all three is to accept the full reality of the nature of man; to accept that reality is to begin to accept the remedies available for not only soul and body but also for our spirits.

The stronghold of our mind that works against us as we explore faith and try to yield to our spirit is called unbelief.

Unbelief as a stronghold can sound like reason. Your thinking will focus on the reasons something is not possible or at least not probable. "Reasonable" explanations will invite you to believe them rather than the "impossible" word of the Lord.

We are very susceptible to this thinking because of our culture. Even in the church, we have a Greek mindset which rests heavily upon logic and theoretical understandings based in materialism.

The scriptures warn us not to lean on our own understanding but to acknowledge God in all things [Prov. 3:5]. We must learn to "think" with our spirits and place our minds in the proper order under the authority of the Holy Spirit [Rom. 8:6].

This is not to suggest that we should stop thinking—quite the opposite! We must think even harder. We should not fear to examine our own thoughts and have enough courage to see the places we may be biased or culture- bound or simply wrong.

We must learn to have a Hebrew mindset which is based on experience with God (testimony) and not ideas about God (theory).

I have found this simple prayer extremely helpful as a way to bring my Greek mindset under the rule of my spirit:

Thank you, Lord, for giving me such a good mind. Mind, I love you and I honor you. I acknowledge your service to me but I repent for allowing you to rule me.

Spirit, stand up and take your proper place in rulership over my mind and my body. I am a trinity made in the image of God; I will submit to the rule of my spirit as it agrees with the Holy Spirit.

I come into agreement with the government of heaven over my life, purpose and destiny. I say to you, mind, you will serve my spirit in Jesus' name, Amen.

My shortcut version of this prayer is, "Mind, sit down; spirit, stand up and take authority. I yield to the Holy Spirit."

We need to strengthen our spirits and bring our minds under the authority of heaven if we are to see and hear Jesus or angels or heaven or anything in the supernatural realm. A mind that is constantly critical of these possibilities will not see miracles. The scriptures testify to this.

And He did not do many miracles there because of their **unbelief**. [Matthew 13:58]

Take care...that there not be in any one of you an evil, **unbelieving** heart that falls away from the living God. [Hebrews 3:12]

...they were broken off for their **unbelief**, but you stand by your faith. Do not be conceited... [Romans 11:20]

He appeared to the eleven as they were reclining at the table; and He reproached them for their **unbelief** and hardness of heart, because they had not believed those who had seen Him after He had risen. [Mark 16:14]

So we see that they were not able to enter because of **unbelief** [Hebrews 3:19]

THE ANTIDOTE TO UNBELIEF IS FAITH!!

Faith– from the Greek "pisteuō"- *conviction of the truth of anything, belief; in the New Testament, a conviction or belief respecting man's relationship to God and divine things, generally with the included idea of **trust** and holy fervor born of faith and joined with it.*

Faith must be exercised in order to get stronger. Use it or lose it! We pull on our faith when circumstances do not support whatever the Lord has taught us or promised us. We declare with our mouths what we know to be true based on our trust in the Lord. This is war! The enemy wants you to declare his mindset into every area of your life—his fear, his unbelief, his accusation, his rejection.

Our faith will be weak if we do not settle the issue of trust. We do not believe people we do not trust; so it is with the Lord. I have been very encouraged by an illustration from Graham Cooke on the subject of spiritual growth. Graham explains our need to learn faith with a story about learning to ride a bicycle.

When we are learning to ride a bike, we have training wheels until we feel ready to take the training wheels off. When the wheels come off, whoever is helping us learn to ride will run with us, holding us up for a time until we gain enough momentum that we are riding on our own.

At this point, if we look around and discover that no one is holding us up anymore, we may go a bit wobbly or even fall over.

We were riding on our own until we lost confidence.

The Lord wants us to be able to ride our spiritual bicycle. He will be near us and hold us up until it is time for us to learn to ride without training wheels. When He lets go, He is inviting us to trust Him. We learn to pull on our faith that He will be there if we fall but He is confident that we can do this.

Jesus…said, "Daughter, take courage; your **faith** has made you well." [Matthew 9:22]

Then He touched their eyes, saying, " It shall be done to you according to your **faith**." [Matthew 9:29]

Then Jesus said to her, "O woman, your **faith** is great; it shall be done for you as you wish." [Matthew 15:28]

Jesus answered and said to them, "Truly I say to you, if you have **faith** and do not doubt, you will not only do what was done to the fig tree, but even if you say to this mountain, 'Be taken up and cast into the sea,' it will happen. [Matthew 21:21]

And He said to the woman, "Your **faith** has saved you; go in peace." [Luke 7:50]

Paul…when he had fixed his gaze on him…had seen that he had **faith** to be made well, [Acts 14:9]

For in it the righteousness of God is revealed from **faith** to **faith**; as it is written, "but the righteous man shall live by **faith**." [Rom. 1:17]

…whatever is not from **faith** is sin. [Rom. 14:23]

for we walk by **faith**, not by sight... [2 Cor. 5:7]

Test yourselves to see if you are in the **faith**; examine yourselves! [2 Cor. 13:5]

the righteous man shall live by **faith**. [Gal. 3:11]

Fight the good fight of **faith**; take hold of the eternal life to which you were called...[1 Timothy 6:12]

Now **faith** is the assurance of things hoped for, the conviction of things not seen. [Heb. 11:1]

By **faith** we understand that the worlds were prepared by the word of God [Heb. 11:3]

By faith Enoch was taken up so that he would not see death; and he was not found because God took him up; for he obtained the witness that before his being taken up he was pleasing to God. [Heb. 11:5]

We can learn to trust Him. He wants us to learn. Since the just shall live by faith[26] and it is impossible to please God without faith,[27] it is critical to our walk to settle the issue of faith in Him.

He either loves you or He doesn't; He's either trustworthy or He isn't. The enemy of our soul does not want us to trust God. He knows the power of faith. It is time for us to learn what our enemy already knows!

---

26 Galatians 3:11
27 Hebrews 11:6

ASK YOURSELF:

1. Do you find it difficult to believe in things you do not see?

   _____

   _____

   _____

   _____

2. Name some things that you do believe in even though they are invisible.

   _____

   _____

   _____

   _____

3. Why do you think that God the Father meets us through experiences that are difficult to quantify?

   _____

   _____

   _____

   _____

4. What are your thoughts on Hebrews 11:1? "Now faith is the substance of things hoped for, the evidence of things **not seen**."

   _____

   _____

   _____

   _____

HEBREWS 4:12 PRAYER

Your soul must come under the rule of your spirit. We pray for our spirit man to rise up and take its proper place. This is a prayer to tear up all of the soul's record, all of its testimony, influence, all of its power, its mandate, all control, dominion and authority:

Father, forgive me for failing to walk in the provision of Hebrews 4:12 that your word is sharper than any two edged sword, dividing my soul and my spirit. I choose today to apply this truth and make it my own by faith.

In the name of Yeshua, I take the word of God and by faith, I force it in between my soul and spirit. I speak to the ties to my soul that have fed off my spirit to give my soul power to rule. I sever this cord of supply so that my spirit man will stand.

I declare I am a spirit being that has a soul that lives in a physical body.

Today, I decree to my soul: bow down before the kingdom of God. I take you into the courtroom of God and I make you bow down to the judicial system of my spirit man to the government of my spirit.

You will be changed as my spirit engages with the glory realm of heaven and you will bow down to my spirit and serve it today. Soul, I will not serve you any longer. In the name of Yeshua, Amen![28]

---

28 This prayer is a prayer by Mike Parsons offered here with some minor edits

THE STRONGHOLD OF ACCUSATION

"Then I heard a loud voice in heaven, saying, 'Now the salvation, and the power, and the kingdom (dominion, reign) of our God, and the authority of His Christ have come; for the accuser of our [believing] brothers and sisters has been thrown down [at last], he who accuses them and keeps bringing charges [of sinful behavior] against them before our God day and night.' "

[Revelations 12:10 AMP]

Mark had an exhausting conversation going on inside his head at all times. If someone confided in him about a shortcoming or something they were struggling with, Mark would hear, "You are guilty of that too; in fact, you are much worse."

If he heard a sermon at church about some sort of sin— it didn't matter which sort—he was sure the minister was talking about him. Mark imagined that he was being humble and teachable. "I am willing to look at my own behavior and to admit I may be wrong," he would often think; but, in fact, Mark was paralyzed by the constant criticism of his inner voice.

The bad behavior of other people became Mark's fault. "I should've said something," he would think. "If I had been paying attention, maybe I could have prevented this."

Mark was a kind person and people often took advantage of him. He would never blame them for their treachery, though; it was easier for him to find fault with himself. "I should have known better; everyone else could see this coming. I am terrible at reading people," he would reason, "You would think I would know by now when someone's motivations are not pure. I am always getting hurt but it's my own fault."

No matter what the circumstance, no matter how far from Mark's life, he could always manage to find a way to accept his share of the blame. If the national news carried headlines of crooked politicians, Mark's thoughts would turn to the responsibility of the voter and he would conclude that he was not a very well-informed person; therefore, these leaders that disappointed us were in power because of his laziness.

If there was news of violence in faraway cities, Mark would conclude that people needed to understand each other better. Since he was a busy person who often didn't take the time to listen to others, he concluded that society's ills were as much his fault as anyone's.

Whenever international news indicated that people did not like Americans, Mark understood. "When I travel," he thought, "I do not often take the time to learn the language of the country I am visiting. This must make me seem rude. It's no wonder that Americans are not well-liked if I am the example that others encounter."

*   *   *

To the person who has never encountered the stronghold of accusation, this thinking seems ridiculous; but for Mark and for those who, like him, live under the tyranny of accusation, this torturous, paralyzing, discouraging inner monologue is a way of life.

In fact, those who are in agreement with the stronghold of accusation believe that to think this way is virtuous.

Remember that one of the features of a stronghold is that even though it is a lie, it seems perfectly true. The best lies have in them elements of truth; this is what makes it difficult to detect the part that is untrue.

A compassionate, secure and mature person would also try to consider their own shortcomings when evaluating human conflict. The difference between honest self-evaluation and an inner voice of accusation is that the accused person will never conclude that they have no responsibility in a matter.

No matter what mental gymnastics they must perform, a person with a stronghold of accusation will conclude that everything is ultimately their responsibility. Even if you are having a discussion about historical events which happened before the person was born, they will find a way to take responsibility by saying something like, "If I were there I would have made the same decision therefore it is much my fault as anyone who was alive at the time."

The problem with accusation is the turmoil and fear that results from such thinking. Guilt is always crouching at the door. Accusation separates us from our true identity and robs us of our peace.

Accusation invites us to agree with condemning judgments.

A constant habit of agreeing with condemning judgments about ourselves easily becomes a habit of agreeing with condemning judgments about others. In this way, accusation divides us— separating us from ourselves, from our family, friends and the rest of the community.

Accusation also distorts our image of YHWH.[29] He becomes critical, judgmental, impossible to please and very distant from us. It is easy to imagine that YHWH is disappointed with us when a critical, condemning voice is constantly repeating this lie.

When we agree with the accusation that we don't measure up to YHWH's standard and, therefore, YHWH is disappointed in us, it is easy to become defensive and even critical of YHWH. After all, we are all doing our best aren't we? In this way, the stronghold of accusation directs itself toward YHWH suggesting that he is at least unreasonable if not altogether unjust.

With suspicion, judgment and condemnation directed toward our

---

29 YHWH, the **tetragrammaton**, meaning "[consisting of] four letters", יהוה in Hebrew and **YHWH** in Latin script, is the four-letter biblical name of the God of Israel.
The books of the **Torah** and the rest of the Hebrew Bible (with the exception of Esther, and Song of Songs) contain this Hebrew name.

Religiously observant Jews and those who follow conservative Jewish traditions do not pronounce יהוה, nor do they read aloud transliterated forms such as *Yahweh*; instead the word is substituted with a different term, whether used to address or to refer to the God of Israel. When you see the written form 'G_d', it is a sign of respect for the name—although it should be noted that 'God' is not His name. His name is YHWH.

Hebrew is read from right to left so the spelling of the sacred name, יהוה, is yod, hei, vav, hei. Letters in Hebrew also have a story attached to them because ancient Hebrew was a pictographic language like Egyptian hieroglyphics.

The story of the name YHWH is a beautiful foretelling of His plans and purposes! "Hand, behold, nail, behold" is the literal rendering of 'Yod, Hei, Vav, Hei'.

neighbor, toward ourselves, and toward YHWH, we are easy to defeat. Our choice seems to be, once again, to give up or to change the standard.

Giving up leads us to cynicism; changing the standard leads us to hypocrisy. What shall we do? Thankfully, defeating accusation is simpler than it seems. Before we discuss the strategies for defeating accusation, let's lay a foundation from Scripture in order to fully understand why this stronghold is so deadly.

Accusations against YHWH

Satan, whose name means "adversary," began by accusing YHWH of unrighteousness in the Garden. Satan accused YHWH to Eve in order to separate her from YHWH by drawing her into deception and temptation to sow doubt about YHWH's Word.[30]

Accusations against Jesus

Satan used many people to accuse Jesus, even in His innocence of any sinful breach of the Law.[31]

Accusations against mankind

Satan accuses mankind of unrighteousness. Satan is the accuser of the brethren, holding against them every violation of the Law.[32]

We are meant to be a united Body, loving one another as He loves us. God loved us first, when we were still in our sin—unrepentant, unredeemed. No matter what we have done, He is still able to love us. Satan is a deceiver, a tempter, a destroyer and an accuser. These are the methods of the kingdom of darkness.

---

30 Genesis 3:4–5
31 Isaiah 53:3–5; Matt 27:37; 1 Peter 2:21–23; Luke 6:7
32 Job 2:3–5; Rev. 12:10–12

Here is an easy way to know the difference between accusation and the voice of the Holy Spirit working through "conviction":[33]

Condemnation	Conviction
accuses	explains
attacks our person (you are bad)	targets our behavior
feels heavy	feels light
brings darkness	enlightens
spreads confusion	brings clarity
brings rejection	brings grace and mercy
fruitless introspection	fruitful objectivity
powerlessness/hopelessness	power to confess
leads to feeling worthless	leads to repentance
brings us into more bondage	leads us into more freedom

Accusation is the same as condemnation. This is different from conviction which is the work of the Holy Spirit bringing us to repentance.

Learn to pay attention to critical thoughts inside of you. Don't agree with judgmental ideas and attitudes about others. Tools: intercede for the other person. Separate them from the sin.

When accused, what should you do? Go to God; see if there is true guilt. If there is, then repent and get the matter right with God and with the person.[34] If there isn't, forgive them for accusing you and stay in fellowship with God. Ask God to protect and defend you and clear your name.[35]

---

33 Based on Healing Streams Ministry course by Rev. Steve Evans
34 Galatians 6:1
35 Psalm 59

Do not trust your feelings—trust His Word. As soon as we repent, God forgives, but accusing spirits keep trying to block any sense of grace. Know the truth—don't try to feel it—and take your peace back.

Watch out for: distrust, suspicion, being easily offended, envy/jealousy, exaggerating faults of others or oneself, gossip, misunderstandings, judging/excusing, noticing faults too regularly.

Just because we have a thought about ourselves or others doesn't mean it is true or that we have to go on thinking it. If you are having a troubling thought, try thinking something different.

Accusation is one of those lies that can paralyze you.

The Holy Spirit comes to lead us and guide us and to help us when we are off the path. The sin in our life is dealt with by the Holy Spirit as we listen to him and agree with him and come to repentance. The Holy Spirit loves us and he is cheerful and he is optimistic. He has a good sense of humor.

The enemy has another way of pointing out sin. He wants us to look at sin from his point of view. "Look at what you did. I can't believe you are still doing that. I can't believe you're not better than this. Why bother? You can't keep asking God to forgive you of this over and over. You know you're sick of yourself so of course God is sick of you. Just give up. You don't deserve forgiveness. You'll never be any better."

This voice is discouraging, negative, and listening to it will bring you to failure and defeat. It does contain truth – every good lie contains truth – but it's not the whole truth. The Lord doesn't speak to us this way. When he says let us lay aside the sin which so easily entangles us[36] he actually gives us a way to lay it aside. The word says that there is no temptation that comes our way for which he does not give a way of escape.[37] We don't often take the way of escape because we don't understand what that looks like.

We think, "I see that this is wrong and I should stop doing it." If I stop doing It, I have repented. Then we 'white knuckle it' and stop the behavior for a while only to fall back into the same sin and come under the same condemnation. We think that's all the power we have. If the Holy Spirit is inside of us, He will give us the strength to stop behaving badly. But this isn't the fullness of our authority. This is only our natural understanding of how to deal with sin. We actually have a much greater authority and a greater means to address sin.

AUTHORITY

The truth is, we have legislative authority. We have the authority of the court behind the power of the judge of the universe on our side and we have a legal means to answer everything that comes against us if we will use it.

There are two main ways for us individually to come into our full authority in a court. One way is to acknowledge and understand and apply the blood of Jesus to answer our individual sin. The other way is to acknowledge and understand and apply the blood of Jesus to answer the sin in our bloodline.

---

36 Hebrews 12:1
37 1 Corinthians 10:13

It is no accident that blood is the means by which the Lord answers every sin. Blood 'speaks' and YHWH hears. The first spilled blood in the earth – the blood of Abel – cried out from the earth and called for justice. The Lord said to Cain, "Your brother's blood cries out to me from the earth."[38] All the blood spilled in the earth from that date to this has cried out for justice.

When Jesus spilled his blood, the answer was given. The Scripture says, "His blood speaks a better word."[39] The blood of Jesus is the answer for every sin but the blood of Jesus is only shed in a theoretical way if we leave it up there on the cross.

We actually have to receive the blood. Jesus said, "Unless you eat my body and drink my blood, you will not have life...For my body is real food for your spirit and my blood is real drink. The one who eats my body and drinks my blood lives in me and I live in him."[40]

That's the level of intimacy that He is after; that's the level of oneness that He is looking for. When we come to Jesus and eat His body and drink His blood, His body and His blood become a part of us. Jesus' blood has become a part of us and we have become a part of Him.

We receive the blood of Jesus and we come into the heavenly court and we ask for all sin to be forgiven through the blood. We accept responsibility for it, we repent and we bring it under the blood. We ask for it to be judged under and through the blood of Jesus. And we ask to be separated from the sin. We ask for the Father to sever any covenantal commitment that we have made to any sin in our life. And that's how we deal with personal sin.

---

38 Genesis 4:10
39 Hebrews 12:24
40 John 6:53–56

Generation sin—sin in our bloodline—can still hinder us even when we have personally come under the blood of Jesus so we can't neglect our generations. We have to go under the mercy covenant and carry all our generations in and carry in the sin of our fathers.[41] Daniel and Nehemiah repented for the sins of their fathers in the Old Testament and Peter spoke of the promise of the Holy Spirit as a promise that was not just for this generation but also for our fathers and for our sons and for future generations.[42]

The Scriptures testify that YHWH sees man in terms of generations and family lines. He does not limit His work to one generation and His promises are multigenerational.[43] When the Scripture says He is looking for a man to 'stand in the gap', that refers to any person in any generation who is willing to bring the sins of the generations into repentance under the sacrificial blood.

Therefore, we repent individually and we also repent for generational iniquity.[44] In this way, we thwart the accuser's plan to limit the abundant promises of YHWH to bless us and bring the increase of His kingdom in and through our lives.

If accusation is speaking to you, shame will rule you and you will be paralyzed. When the Holy Spirit is speaking, you are invited into your future and given a way to get there. You have weapons and tools; you have standing in the court.

Psalm 139 says that all of this is written in our 'book'.[45] The book of my time on the earth is limited to the testimonies of the earth—of what I'm walking in here on earth.

---

41 Daniel 9:4–23; Nehemiah 1:4–11
42 Joel 2:28
43 Genesis 9:12
44 Isaiah 59:2
45 Psalms 139:16

ASK YOURSELF:

1. What is the voice of accusation accusing you of today?

   _____

   _____

   _____

   _____

2. Explain why you believe it is true.

   _____

   _____

   _____

   _____

3. How do you think Father God sees the situation?

   _____

   _____

   _____

   _____

4. How would your thinking change if you were to see from YHWH's perspective?

   _____

   _____

   _____

   _____

TAKE IT TO COURT!

I ask that a heavenly court be convened to hear the evidence in the matter of accusation in my generations and my own life. I thank You, Lord, that I can enter your court today. I come not in my own righteousness, but in the righteousness of Yeshua, my Lord and Savior. I come under the covering of the word of God and the blood of Yeshua.

By faith, Lord, I step into your presence and make my petition. Lord, I ask for a discovery of all my accusers. I ask that they be brought into court bound with chains according to Psalm149 and that their lips be mute according to Psalm 31. I acknowledge these accusations as my own sin; I accept responsibility for every time I knowingly and unknowingly agreed with accusation.

I repent for agreeing with accusation, for believing lies and I receive the blood of Jesus over my spirit, soul and body to dissolve all covenants with accusation in me and my generations.

I ask You, Father, to judge me now according to the dispensation of Messiah; I ask You also to judge everything outside of my covering with the same judgment and to judge my accusers with the same judgment.

I ask for restitution and compensation for everything that they have stolen from me and my ancestors and family. I also ask for divorce papers, restraining orders and restraints on the spirits responsible for all of this and I ask that they be kept away from me and my family, loved ones and dear ones.

I receive these papers in my spirit and ask for them to be recorded in my book. By faith, Lord, I ascend into the place of your presence and I step onto the sea of glass. I release everything onto the sea of glass just as in Revelation 4:10 the 24 elders cast their crowns before you in an act of worship and honor. I abandon myself to you in holy reverence and awe. I say with those around the throne, "Holy are you, YHWH!"

I step out of the place of your presence into this world and I release the mandate from YHWH into this atmosphere and I ask for angelic help in administrating your mandate into the earth in Jesus' name.

HIGH PLACES (TRADING FLOORS)

The "high places" spoken of in the Old Testament are places of worship given to false gods (demon spirits). These are places of commerce in the spirit world known as "trading floors" Israel sacrificed on these altars when they did not know and believe that YHWH was faithful. It was an act of rebellion and God judged them for it.

You might wonder what relevance ancient altars have in a conversation about addressing strongholds. The fact is, when we do not believe the promises of God, we make a choice. It is not a neutral choice to refuse to believe YHWH. Whether we acknowledge Him or not, the laws of the universe still apply.

I may choose to disbelieve gravity but it will apply to me nevertheless. If I choose to disregard YHWH, my faith will be in someone or something else. Think about it.

Are you self sufficient? Don't need anybody or any belief system? You have faith in yourself. This is a kind of worship. In the spirit realm, you are making a trade at the altar of self. It is worship at the high places.

Is it a religious system you trust? Perhaps you believe in the way your parents raised you or in what your church teaches. These traditions are fine until they interfere with the leading of the Holy Spirit.

Sooner or later, there will be a conflict and you will have to choose. It is the Lord's intention to call us to Himself. If we choose our belief system over the voice of the Lord, our faith is in the traditions of men. We are making a trade on an altar of religion.

The sacrifice we make is one of trust. We place our trust on the altar of a false promise or a false reality. To be free, we must tear down the high places and remove the sacrifices from the altars.

We must stop trusting the lies and begin trusting YHWH.

When we do business with the enemy, we literally exchange something of our own for provision from the kingdom of darkness. We do this in ignorance, mostly, but we may also make a conscious trade using rationalization to cover our choice. We may stubbornly refuse to believe truth once this choice has been made.

A believer I know (let's call him Randy) was spiritually stuck. Randy said he believed he was demonized and he wanted deliverance but didn't think it would "do any good". After asking some questions, the story he gave was a good example of this phenomenon of trading floors.

A female friend who Randy considered "spiritual" told him he had welcomed 'a darkness' into his life. She also said that it wouldn't leave because it had been with Randy so long it had become a part of him.

Since we know that Jesus is Lord of all and that no power on earth or in heaven can match the power of Jesus, we know that no darkness can stand against the light of His presence. Randy believed his friend instead of the clear word of scripture.

As long as this brother believed that the darkness was a part of him and would not leave, he received according to his faith. He was making a sacrifice of trust on a demonic altar.

The issue was further complicated by a secondary trade on an altar of lust. This "spiritual" sister had sexual intercourse with Randy. He was committed to her explanation that it was the darkness in him that kept her from getting closer.

The trading floor or altar of lust is a common place of worship for men and women of every generation. There, a person makes a trade similar to the one made in ancient pagan temples where temple prostitution was common.

When blood and seed is offered on an altar of worship, a person's DNA is made available to the demonic realm. This is very powerful since trading in DNA is the same sort of trade made in the blood sacrifice of Jesus. The scriptures say that the blood "speaks".[46]

In order to get free, Randy needs to repent by removing the sacrifice from the altar of deception while returning it to the altar of the Lord. We make ourselves living sacrifices according to the book of

---

46   Hebrews 12:24 and Genesis 4:10

Romans.[47] All this brother needs to do is change his focus. Turn into Jesus and away from any lie about his identity. Remove the trust he has placed on the wrong altar and bring his trust as an offering to the Lord. This is true repentance.

There was a renewal song in the 1970's called "Turn Your Eyes Upon Jesus". It was good advice!

Every illegal trade we have made on altars of deception can be addressed through repentance. Just ask the Holy Spirit to show you where your sacrifices have been made. Then remove them.

Scriptures about the High Places:
1 Kings 3:2,3;12:31;14:23; 2 Kings 12:3; 14:4; 15:4,35; 16:4; 17:9,11,32; 18:4; 21:3;23:20; 2 Chronicles 20:33; 2 Sam 1:9; Ps 78:58; Jer 19:5; Ezekiel 16:39

---

47 Rom. 12:1

PRAYER OVER THE TRADING FLOORS/HIGH PLACES

Repent of making sacrifices to demonic altars:

Recognize:
1. Ask the Lord to show you any illegal trades with which you have been engaged.

Responsibility and Repent:
2. Father, I have traded with this demonic spirit [name it (ex. Fear, lust, unbelief, bitterness)] and given myself over to it and empowered it to rule in my life and given it the capacity and ability to administrate its desire through me. I repent and receive the blood of Jesus to cancel every contract, every covenant I have made with this lie.

Remove:
3. Father, by faith, I receive the blood of Jesus Christ that cleanses me from false trading and the power that agreement has had over me. I tear down ancient altars from this trading floor and I remove my name from these altars.

Renounce/Resist:
4. Lord, today I decree that I will not trade with it any longer. My desire is to trade in your presence. Today, Lord, whatever I have traded, by faith, I take that back [ask the Lord to show you what you have traded]. I take it off the trading floor of the enemy and I break my agreement with [name the demonic spirit]. I tear up any former contracts or agreements and cancel them by covering them with the blood of Jesus.

Restore:

5. By faith, Lord, I take a step forward into your presence; I ascend into the place of your presence and by faith I step onto the sea of glass. I release onto the sea of glass the stuff that I have traded and I trade it for your kingdom, Lord, that out of the realm of heaven I would receive your kingdom.

6. Today, Lord, I go up into my mountain by faith and I take the measure of your kingdom for which I have made a trade and I put it into my mountain in my life and I descend into your presence.

7. I step out of the place of your presence into this world and I release that mandate from God into this atmosphere. I ask for all angelic help to carry out my mandate, in Jesus' name.

Inside the image: WE ARE THE WAY THE TRUTH AND THE LIFE COME AND JOIN US (MEMBERS ONLY)

THE STRONGHOLD OF RELIGION

Imagine I own a vehicle and you do not. We make a plan to do something in the next town over—a town that is five miles away. If I say, "Meet me there in ten minutes" but then I drive off and leave you to get there on foot, I have made a request that you cannot carry out.

You may try to borrow someone else's vehicle. You may try to obtain a vehicle of your own. You may begin the journey on foot but you will not make it there in ten minutes.

My words will frustrate you. You will be frustrated by your inability to carry out the request and frustrated by the request itself. Before long, you will begin to question your understanding of the request. You may begin to question my character and my motivations.

"Maybe I misunderstood. Why would anyone invite me to do something with them and then drive off and leave me standing there?" You will draw the very natural conclusion that either you didn't hear me right or I am clueless about the nature of time and space and human limitation. You dismiss my invitation as impractical nonsense.

Now suppose that someone gives you a book in which you find all sorts of directions for your destination. In the book are the stories of many people who tried to take the same journey you want to take. Some people made it there, some people did not. You begin to get the idea that going to the next town is more important than you realized.

This inspires you to read the book cover to cover. You love the book but it frustrates you. At different times, while reading the stories of others who took the journey, you try to do what they did but your journey does not go the same way. And you still do not have a vehicle.

Suppose you meet others who are trying to take this journey. These others gather regularly to talk about the journey and encourage each other. They share strategies to make the journey easier; they suggest goals that you can set along the way to encourage you in your journey.

They talk about the book when they meet together. They tell you not to worry if you can't do what you see others in the book doing. The book is very old, they say, and the people in it are long dead. They don't understand what it's like to make this journey today. If they were alive today, they would think like we think and the story of their journey would be different.

Also, much of the book is symbolic. We are not meant to believe every word. Only the very young or the very foolish believe every word. Much of the book is poetry and no one tries to imitate poetry. Your frustration, they assert, is because of your lack of understanding.

These answers satisfy you. They agree with your experience. After all, you did try to make the journey the way you saw it done in the book but nothing came of it. In the back of your mind, you know that you are missing something but you conclude that you were not meant to understand everything so you accept what you do not know and you continue to walk in the only way you know how to walk.

This describes the way many believers think about their spiritual life. After initially being inspired by an invitation to something greater than ourselves, we find the way confusing and difficult and frustrating. We look around and we don't see anyone walking in a way we want to imitate.

We conclude that we must have misunderstood. Our choices seem to be either to abandon the journey or to redefine it. Too many of us choose the latter. When we redefine the journey, we radically change the purposes and the plan of God.

When we try to define the journey according to our own understanding, we are eating from the tree of the knowledge of good and evil.[48] We are practicing religion.

Jesus did not come to establish another religion! The mystery of the gospel is this: Jesus doesn't just say, "Follow me," he says, "You must die so that I may live. I will send the same Spirit that raised me from the dead[49] to dwell in you. This Spirit will teach, train, lead, guide, comfort and remind you of everything I said— even

---

48 Genesis 2:17
49 Romans 8:11

tell you what is going to happen in the future.[50] This Spirit will completely transform your thinking until you have my mind in place of your own.[51]"

The Spirit of God, the third person of the trinity, comes to dwell in us so that we might be able to do the impossible. This is meant to be a game changer.

Abbie's story:

Abbie grew up in the church. She could not remember a time when she wasn't helping. She enjoyed volunteering and at one time or another had given her time and talent to almost every need—the choir, the youth group, Sunday school, organizing retreats, making hospital visits, fundraisers, vacation Bible schools, new members covered dish dinners, the soup kitchen, and endless numbers of committees. She was organized and cheerful and she didn't mind the extra time it took to help out. When Abbie heard messages about intimacy with the Lord, she thought such things were for others—the "Marys" of the body of Christ, not the "Marthas". Abbie knew she was a "Martha".

In fact, she took pride in her service. She felt valuable to the work of the church. "If everyone sat around meditating like Mary, how would anything ever get done? Maybe we don't get the credit we deserve but we know who is doing the 'heavy lifting'", she reasoned. Abbie had developed a "works" mentality—a performance mindset.

It was a short leap from taking pride in her work to feeling that the work justified her. Soon, she felt the most important part of her relationship to God was the service she rendered. As time went on,

---

50 John 16:13
51 1 Corinthians 2:16

Abbie felt insignificant without work to do for God.

It was at this point in her walk with God that He interrupted her path. Abbie's husband got a job offer and the couple chose to move away from the place she had grown comfortable.

The search for a new church was difficult for Abbie. Every place they went did not feel like "home". She was lonely and depressed about church and she felt guilty that she wasn't doing anything for God.

One week, she decided to spend Sunday morning at home reading her Bible and praying. As she sat quietly, the Lord spoke. "What are you doing, Abbie?"

"I think I am mourning, Lord. I miss my old church and my friends and the feeling of being useful to You, Lord," Abbie responded.

"I don't want you to be useful to me, Abbie," the Lord answered. "I am not interested in your service."

Ouch. This was a difficult truth but she knew it was the voice of the Lord. He was calling her into a more intimate relationship with Him and it scared her.

James' story:

James was a theology buff. He loved to go to prayer meetings so he could check other people's belief systems. If he heard anyone say anything out of alignment with Christian orthodoxy, he would challenge them, often taking over the meeting in order to drive his point home. (His point was usually that they were wrong and he was right.)

If you wanted to be James' friend, you had to believe what James believed. Or you had to hide your disagreement. If any subject came up upon which there was a variety of opinion, James would establish his opinion loudly and communicate that every other view was inferior.

No one wanted to get into a debate with James. It simply wasn't worth it. James was so fully committed to what he "knew" to be true that he defended himself against spiritual growth without even realizing what he was doing. He fed himself a steady diet from the tree of the knowledge of good and evil until he was nearly dead inside.

One day, a brave friend asked James a question that James couldn't answer. "Why are you operating out of your mind instead of out of your spirit?" he asked. This simple question sent James on a journey that eventually freed him from the stronghold of religion.

If you ask him today, he will laugh and tell you, "I was so addicted to religion and to being right!" Now he is willing to embrace mystery and the unknowable; he accepts that God is bigger. His mind is open, his spirit is open and his heart is wide open.

*　　　*　　　*

Life in the Spirit requires us to hear the voice of the Lord. Life in Religion requires only that we learn the rules and obey them. These two ways of living our spiritual lives are not compatible. They are in conflict and in order to mature, a believer must choose between them.

The scriptures teach us that the law kills but the Spirit gives life[52] and that the law is meant for the immature.[53] The gospels give us

---

52 2 Corinthians 3:6
53 Galatians 3:24-25

examples of how religious people can miss the plans and purposes of God because of their focus on the letter of the law.

"You have sent to John, and he has testified to the truth. But the testimony which I receive is not from man, but I say these things so that you may be saved. He was the lamp that was burning and was shining and you were willing to rejoice for a while in his light.

"But the testimony which I have is greater than the testimony of John; for the works which the Father has given Me to accomplish— the very works that I do—testify about Me, that the Father has sent Me.

"And the Father who sent Me, He has testified of Me. You have neither heard His voice at any time nor seen His form. You do not have His word abiding in you, for you do not believe Him whom He sent.

"You search the Scriptures because you think that in them you have eternal life; it is these that testify about Me; and you are unwilling to come to Me so that you may have life. I do not receive glory from men; but I know you, that you do not have the love of God in yourselves. I have come in My Father's name, and you do not receive Me; if another comes in his own name, you will receive him. How can you believe, when you receive glory from one another and you do not seek the glory that is from the one and only God?"

[John 5:33–44]

From the beginning, the choice was between *the tree of the knowledge of good and evil and the tree of life.*[54] Our enemy has always wanted us to eat from the wrong tree. It brings death!

---

54 Genesis 2:16-17

Consider the example of Cain and Abel in the book of Genesis. Abel made a sacrifice of blood from his flock while Cain, who was a tiller of the soil, sacrificed from the ground.[55]

At face value, it seems harmless for Cain to make his sacrifice from the crops he had grown. Why was this unacceptable to God? The answer has to do with obedience. A clear sacrificial system was set in place by God. Blood alone can atone for sin.

When Cain made a different sacrifice, he substituted his own judgment for God's. He ate from the tree of the knowledge of good and evil—the same sin Adam and Eve committed. Abel sacrificed blood (obedience to God based on the tree of life).

Murder
Persecution and murder are in religion!
- Cain slew Abel out of jealousy and self righteousness.
- Saul of Tarsus murdered followers of Jesus out of a righteous interpretation of the law.
- The Pharisees killed Jesus out of a righteous interpretation of the law.
- Some religions endorse the death penalty for breaking religious law.

Persecution
Idealism and perfectionism come from religion!!
- They produce self righteousness, judgment of others and persecution.
- Fear and Pride are at the root.
- Comparison to others is the constant temptation. Insecurity and inferiority drive us to seek God's approval through good works.

---

55 Genesis 4:3

- When others get praised or credited with more gifts or accomplishments than us, the spirit of religion drives us to envy and jealousy.
- Jealousy will drive us to gossip, slander, division, rejection, bitterness, even murder.

THE CULTURE OF HONOR

Why is it so difficult for Christians to get along with each other? Why is there so much suspicion and self-righteous condemnation between the denominations?

It is important to understand that a stronghold of religion inhibits our ability to give honor to one another in the kingdom. Religion separates us with critical thoughts which are competitive in their nature. We find ourselves functioning as "the doctrine police" instead of seeking ways to agree and find common ground.

The truth is, Christians agree on much more than we realize. Virtually all Christian denominations share a basic orthodoxy. With only one or two exceptions, we all agree that Jesus was a real person who walked the earth.

We agree that he was born of a virgin in Bethlehem of Judea in fulfillment of Jewish prophecy concerning a coming Messiah; that he died and rose again, that He is a king of a kingdom that is yet to come and that he will return in bodily form to establish his kingdom on earth.

We accept the redemptive work of the cross, the Godhead as a Trinity and the promise of eternal life. We believe in the value of life, in the human soul and in the existence of good and evil. We agree that it is our responsibility to do good and not evil.

That's a lot of agreement. Our differences seem to be limited to differences in how we interpret the scripture on a few matters: the communion table, church government, the gifts of the Holy Spirit and end times eschatology. There is also the matter of how we view the scriptures themselves (literally true, heavily metaphorical or some combination of those two). Everything else is church culture.

It is interesting to note that we often value and respect other cultures in the kingdom of earth while we regard with suspicion other cultures in the kingdom of heaven. This is a stronghold of religion at work.

Jack Deere and Rick Joyner offer some helpful insights on the spirit of religion which I offer here in addition to a few of my own insights. To lighten it up a bit, think of Jeff Foxworthy's comedy routine "You might be a redneck if..." Remember that laughter—especially laughing at yourself—is a weapon against this stronghold.

You may be in agreement with a spirit of religion if you:

1. are unable to accept correction; "I will only listen to God".
2. use your discernment to tear down.
3. see yourself as appointed to fix others.
4. see more wrong than right with people and churches.
5. keep score/take pride in spiritual life, maturity, disciplines.
6. feel you are more pleasing to God than others.
7. feel overwhelming guilt at failures to meet God's standard.
8. are bossy, overbearing and intolerant when in leadership.
9. view supernatural manifestations as approval from God.
10. are encouraged when your ministry looks better than others'.
11. have a mechanical prayer life; repulsed by emotionalism.
12. do things in order to be noticed by people.
13. use emotionalism as a substitute for the Holy Spirit.
14. glory more in God's past work than in what He is doing now.
15. feel suspicion of new movements, churches, etc.
16. reject spiritual manifestations you do not understand.
17. overreact to carnality and/or sin in the church.
18. are unable to join anything that is not perfect or nearly perfect.
19. are overly paranoid of the religious spirit.

Here are some strategies to get free:

1. Develop a secret relationship with the Lord.
2. Spend time alone with the Lord each day.
3. Study the word for intimacy with Him.
4. Learn who you are in Him.
5. Learn to make mistakes.
6. When you mess up, repent and receive forgiveness.
7. Pray to be filled with the love of the Father.
8. Learn to love your neighbor as the Lord does.
9. Turn criticism into prayer.
10. Avoid martyrdom; learn to say, "no".
11. Get free of rejection and accusation.
12. Labor to enter into rest. [Hebrews 4:11]

ASK YOURSELF:

1. Describe an instance when Holy Spirit told you something that made you uncomfortable.

   _____

   _____

   _____

   _____

2. Describe the last time the Lord showed you that your theology was wrong.

   _____

   _____

   _____

   _____

3. How do you feel when you are asked to be still and remain in the secret place with the Lord?

   _____

   _____

   _____

   _____

4. List three things you have done in secret for which you did not receive any recognition.

   _____

   _____

   _____

   _____

HOW TO TAKE THIS TO COURT:

I ask that a heavenly court be convened to hear the evidence in the matter of religion in my generations and my own life. I thank You, Lord, that I can enter your court today. I come not in my own righteousness, but in the righteousness of Yeshua, my Lord and Savior. I come under the covering of the word of God and in the blood of Yeshua.

By faith, Lord, I step into your presence and make my petition. Lord, I now ask for a discovery of all my accusers. I ask that they be brought into court bound with chains and fetters of iron according to Psalm149 and that their lips be mute according to Psalm 31. I acknowledge these accusations as my own sin; I accept responsibility for every time I knowingly and unknowingly agreed with a spirit of religion, for every time I relied on a form of my own righteousness to satisfy the requirements of the law regarding sin in my life.

I repent for participating in these practices, for believing lies and I receive the blood of Jesus over my spirit, soul and body to dissolve all covenants with evil in me and my generations.

I ask You, Father, to judge me now according to the dispensation of Messiah; I ask You also to judge everything outside of my covering with the same judgment and to judge my accusers with the same judgment.

I ask for restitution and compensation for everything that they have stolen from me and my ancestors and family. I also ask for divorce papers, restraining orders and restraints on the spirits responsible for all of this and I ask that they be kept away from me and my family, loved ones and dear ones.

I receive these papers in my spirit and ask for them to be recorded in my book.

By faith, Lord, I ascend into the place of your presence and I step onto the sea of glass. I make an offering of everything I received today and ask for angelic help to carry out the mandate of repentance in the earth.

THE STRONGHOLD OF BITTERNESS

John was disappointed with his life. He hated his job, hated his house, hated his kids and sometimes he thought he even hated God. His wife divorced him after years of feeling she was always disappointing him. Everyone disappointed John.

His childhood was one big disappointment. He always felt his sister got more attention and more love. His mother died young but John remembered her sadness. She was always sighing.

His dad was too busy to pay much attention to John and when he did, he didn't have much patience. John remembered the drinking and the rages. He hated his father.

Although he swore he'd never be anything like his "old man", John started drinking heavily at forty. He was angry and had outbursts that made his ex-wife fear for the safety of their children. Visitation was renegotiated and John saw them only under supervision.

It was a relief to John. He only wanted to be left alone.

One night, in a drunken stupor, John lay down in the middle of a road. A passing truck didn't see him in time. He was killed when the truck swerved to avoid him and ran over his chest, crushing John's heart.

No one in John's family knew if he had committed suicide or if his death was an accident.

*　　*　　*

John's story is the story of bitterness working generationally. His dad, his mother, even John himself showed signs of self-bitterness and bitterness toward others.

John was raised in a household that agreed with bitterness and accepted it as a way of seeing the world. This transferred to John and he began to agree with bitterness himself from the earliest age.

Hebrews 12:14–16 says "Pursue peace with all people, and holiness, without which no one will see the Lord: looking carefully lest anyone fall short of the grace of God; lest any root of bitterness springing up cause trouble, and by this many become defiled..."

Grudges do bad things to our bodies, hearts, minds and spirits. The root of bitterness defiles us and then it defiles those who make contact with us.

John's parents did not know that they were defiling their son but they were. Because they did not check their own bitterness, that bitterness had the power to affect others— especially John.

This is a problem we see on a grand scale in our world today. Mothers and fathers teach their children to hate and the children grow up not only hating but teaching their own children to hate until entire cultures, races and religions can find no common ground. Blacks against whites; Muslims against Jews; the poor against the rich; one political party hates another; one gender hates another; one sexual orientation hates another— it is an epidemic of bitterness.

What can be done? As we used to say in the 1960s, "You are either part of the problem or part of the solution." To become part of the solution is to become aware of all the ways bitterness has been taught to each of us. As believers, we must repent and tear down the stronghold of bitterness in our own heart.

Bitterness begins rather small with simple unforgiveness but it will grow into something deadly if unchecked. There are seven degrees of bitterness. The first is choosing not to forgive when offended or when we get our feelings hurt or when someone wrongs us. This is called "unforgiveness".

The second degree of bitterness is resentment. We have moved into resentment when we begin to rehearse our grudges. When we keep a record of wrongs and when we can recite the wrongs that others have committed against us we are practicing resentment.

Retaliation follows resentment. Once we begin to rehearse grudges it isn't long before we begin to consider ways to get even with the person or persons who have wronged us. As Christians, we know that "vengeance belongs to the Lord"[56] so we are more likely to get even by criticism or passive aggressive behavior.

---

56 Romans 12:19

Once we have established our agreement with bitterness by choosing unforgiveness, resentment, and retaliation, a fourth degree of bitterness will show up—anger and wrath. This is a sudden surge of emotion which may manifest as yelling, screaming, threatening and name-calling.

Anger itself is not sin. The Bible tells us to "be angry but do not sin in your anger".[57] Jesus himself was angry so we can conclude that there is a place and a time for anger. The anger of bitterness is not a righteous anger. It has as its object a person or a group. We are told that "our battle is not against flesh and blood but against powers and rulers in heavenly places". **Righteous anger is focused on the spiritual source whereas unrighteous anger is focused on the human person.**

The fifth degree of bitterness is hatred. Hatred manifests as exclusion, rejection, strong disliking, intense ill will, despising and detesting. Individuals and groups prefer to isolate themselves from those who are the object of their bitterness. This is highly dangerous and injurious.

Once isolated from those who we hate, it is too easy to justify violence against them. Violence is the sixth degree of bitterness. When hatred becomes violent, people are lashing out wanting to see harm come to another because of the harm (either real or imagined) done to them.

Unless we repent of bitterness in its early stages, murder is the deadly result. As believers, we will gossip and slander and back-bite rather than commit the crime of murder but the destructive spirit is the same. Whether we wish others dead or take steps to ensure their mortal demise—the spirit is the same.

---

57 Ephesians 4:26

These are the manifestations of bitterness when directed outward toward others but bitterness can also be directed against oneself.

We might find it difficult to forgive ourselves when we make mistakes (unforgiveness). We may find ourselves rehearsing our failures in our minds going over and over them unable to let things go (resentment).

We think of ways to punish ourselves for our failings (retaliation) or become increasingly angry with ourselves while we engage in inner monologues of self-rejection and self-hatred (anger and wrath; hatred). Depression is anger turned inward. When we fail to resolve bitterness against the self and it grows in degree, depression will almost certainly become an issue.

Our wish to do harm to ourselves can manifest as cutting behavior or self- mutilation (violence). Finally, bitterness turned inward may find its ultimate expression in suicide (self-murder).

7 degrees of bitterness[58]

1. Un-forgiveness—choosing not to let go of hurt, offenses, or wrongs.
2. Resentment—choosing to "re-feel" old offenses; keeping a record of wrongs.
3. Retaliation—getting even by criticism, passive aggressive behavior, etc.
4. Anger and wrath—sudden surge, goes out to the other person or down upon oneself.
5. Hatred—detesting, despising, strong disliking, intense ill will, rejection and exclusion.
6. Violence—wanting to see harm come to another, desiring to lash out or hurt back.

---

58 Seven Degrees of Bitterness are based on Pleasant Valley Church's Seminar "For Your Life" by Pastor Henry Wright

7. Murder—with the tongue, or in the heart, or by criminal act; wishing them dead.

The origin of a stronghold of bitterness may be hurt or trauma from wrongs done to us in our past. Trauma can open the way to accusations by our invisible enemy and accusation can go two ways.

It can either lead to self-condemnation and bitterness against the self or it can lead to judgment—bitterness against others (including God).

The temptation to judgment

The enemy seeks to turn discernment into bitter judgment and bind the sinner to the sin. Bitter judgment is contrary to what Jesus suffered at the cross. Bitter judgment is fruit from the tree of the knowledge of good and evil.

The necessity of forgiveness

Forgiveness is the opposite of bitter judgment; it releases/separates the sinner from the sin. Forgiveness is why Jesus went to the cross. Forgiveness is the very nature of God in us.

Forgiveness is the key to the Kingdom of God (Matt. 16:18–20; John 20:21–23). The key that Peter was given, as with all of us, is the ability, in the Holy Spirit's power, to bind and loose. We are to loose sinners from their sins and bind the enemy. But when we bind sinners to their sins, we loose the enemy instead.

Biblical incentive to forgive

Mark 11:25 "And *whenever you stand praying, if you have anything against anyone, forgive him,* that your Father in heaven may also forgive you your trespasses. But if you do not forgive, neither will your Father in heaven forgive your trespasses."

It's important to discuss here the issue of forgiving oneself. It is a popular teaching today that we must forgive ourselves; it seems true since self- bitterness is such a scourge. The problem is that **it is not Biblical for me to forgive myself.**

When I see sin in my life, the proper response is repentance. From the position of a repented heart, I must sometimes work to receive the forgiveness purchased for me at the cross—especially if the accuser is very active—but there is no forgiveness without repentance. If I continually jump to the step of forgiveness without first repenting, I will develop what the Bible calls a 'seared' conscience.

The way of repentance

Every change in our heart will be accomplished through repentance. Repentance is not the same as feeling bad or sorrowing over sin. We may sorrow over sin but emotions are not necessary in order to accomplish repentance.

We have been taught that repentance simply means 'changing direction' and that is partially true. The more significant meaning of repentance, however, is the priestly meaning.

Repentance is accomplished when we bring the blood of Jesus against our sin or the sin of others and we cancel the effect of sin going forward. This is our high priestly role; every believer is invited to act as a priest of the sacrifice in order to liberate those who are bound by the effects of sin.[59]

---

59 Hebrews 6:20 Jesus is the "forerunner" of this priesthood

In ancient Israel, the high priest took the blood of the sacrifice and sprinkled it upon the mercy seat. As he did so, he pronounced forgiveness for the sin of the entire nation.

He was charged with preparing his own heart first so that he would be worthy to administrate the sacrifice, but the blood was shed for all. When we function in our role as those who administer the sacrifice, we must first purify ourselves by seeking forgiveness and accepting the blood shed for our sin. We do not neglect the opportunity to bring the blood to bear on the sins of others, however.

As we repent from stronghold thinking, we will accept the blood for our own sin first and then we will apply the blood to those who have sinned against us as well as all of those who have sinned before us. This is a legal matter in the kingdom and it will be carried out in the courts of heaven since the perfect sacrifice was made long ago at the cross.

The acceptance of the blood and the application of the blood to the sin of others is a legal matter now. By faith, we step into the realm of the government of God under the mercy covenant through the veil that was torn and we ask for a hearing on the matter with which we are concerned.

ASK YOURSELF:

1. Are there some things you cannot forgive? List them.

_____

_____

_____

_____

2. How are you at receiving love and forgiveness from the Father?

_____

_____

_____

_____

3. Do you see bitterness in your family?

_____

_____

_____

_____

4. Would you say that a person needs to feel like forgiving before they can forgive? Or is forgiveness a matter of obedience in which we choose to surrender our right to hold on to the sin another has committed?

_____

_____

_____

_____

5. What would happen if everyone chose to forgive?

_____

_____

_____

_____

HERE IS AN EXAMPLE OF A COURT CASE ON THE STRONGHOLD OF BITTERNESS:

Father, I thank you for your mercy and for your justice. Your judgments are true and righteous altogether. I step into the realm of your government under the provision of the blood of Jesus through the veil that has been torn. I thank you for permission to bring the case of bitterness before you now in the heavenly courts.

Lord, I accept responsibility for agreeing with bitterness in any form. I confess my sin to you, Jesus, as my mediator. I ask your word to judge me in this matter under the mercy covenant.

I repent for making a false covenant with bitterness in my heart. I have been slow to forgive; I have kept a record of wrongs; I have imagined ways of retaliating for wrongs committed against me. I have been angry in an unjust way and I have excluded myself from the fellowship of others with whom I have been offended. I have wished for others to be punished and I have gossiped about those who have wronged me.

I repent for all of this and I break agreement with bitterness right now in Jesus name. I bring the blood of Jesus against any covenant I have made illegally and I reject any false joining with any demonic spirit of bitterness.

I join myself to the Lordship and the kingship of Jesus Christ. He is my Savior; he is my Lord and my king.

Father, judge me in this area today—judge in fire, judge in glory, judge in might and power so that I will be made free and liberated from this stronghold.

I choose to become the bride of Christ and I ask for divorce papers from bitterness. I sign those papers and testify with my DNA and the blood of Jesus as two witnesses in the court of Heaven. Amen.

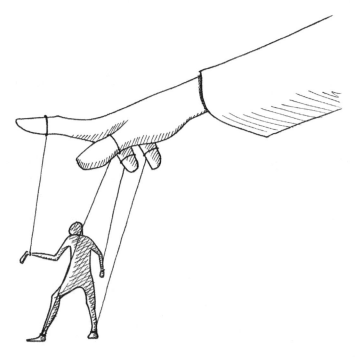

THE STRONGHOLD OF THE OCCULT

Dave was an intelligent and curious student. He was raised in the church but decided early on that although church people seemed sincere, they didn't have any real power. His search for spiritual power led him to research alien phenomenon, astral projection, channeling, hidden knowledge, spiritual science and mysticism.

Soon he began practicing Tarot card reading, lucid dreaming and astral projection. Something real began to happen in his experience. He learned how to travel in the spirit and how to see into the future. His attitude toward Christians became increasingly superior. He felt that Christians were intellectual inferiors who didn't have much intelligence.

His interpretation was that he had tapped into his "God consciousness" and these experiences were the reward for his hard work. For Dave, Jesus was a special ascended class of human being worthy of respect but not his Lord and Savior.

His life went on well for a time but addictions to cigarettes, alcohol and pornography began to take control of him. As his life began to slide into addiction, he became increasingly dissatisfied with his spiritual journey. He couldn't find peace or joy or freedom in any of the practices to which he was so committed.

His heart yearned for something more. Eventually, he turned to Jesus and began to research the claims of Christianity—claims that God is personal rather than an energy blob and that Jesus is God's son who came to bring us peace.

One night, Dave saw how wretched his life had become. More than that, he was hungry to know if Jesus was really the answer. In his desperation, he cried out to Jesus and asking him to reveal himself. What followed was immediate and vivid and more real than anything Dave had yet encountered.

He described a feeling of "holiness" that came upon him and the awareness that "everything in creation was giving praise to Jesus".

Peace and love washed over Dave in liquid waves as he wept at the beauty of God's plan for him.

His heart was wondrously changed. Addictions fell away and a desire to follow Jesus took their place. He began to hear the voice of the Holy Spirit in his heart and a new intimacy with the creator of the universe replaced his lonely alienation.

Dave met Jesus and, in one instant, was changed forever.

"Occult" means hidden or secret. Examples of occult practices in the scriptures include sorcery, witchcraft, divination, idolatry. Supernatural phenomena are not occult; the source of the power is the issue, not the manifestation of power.

The punishment in Israel for participation in occult practices was death. Since God's desire was to guard the nation from all forms of alliance with evil, the physical death of an individual was preferable to the spiritual death which is the result of partnering with demonic spirits.

All forms of witchcraft force us to choose between the legal power of the Holy Spirit and the illegal power of the enemies of God (not the people but the demonic entities). Choosing illegal power makes you an enemy of God. The most urgent cautions against making this choice are offered in the scriptures along with the most extreme consequences.

The scriptures are clear about occult practices:

1. Wickedness of... (1 Sam. 15:23; Isaiah 44:25)
2. Punishment for... (Ex. 22:18; Lev. 20:27; Deut. 13:5
3. To cease... (Ezek. 12:23,24;13:23; Micah 5:12)
4. Denounced... (Isaiah 8:19; Malachi 3:5)
5. Forbidden... (Lev. 19:26–28,31;20:6; Deut. 18:9–14)
6. Diviners will be confounded... (Micah 3:7

If you have participated in any occult activity, the following prayer is an effective prayer of repentance. **This prayer is a good example of how to administrate the blood of Jesus in your role as a priest in the Kingdom Of God.**

ASK YOURSELF:

1. List any occult practices to which you have been exposed.
   Ask the Holy Spirit to help you to see.

   _____

   _____

   _____

   _____

2. Bring your list into the heavenly court so that you can repent
   and ask for the Father's judgment on the matter.

   _____

   _____

   _____

   _____

HOW TO TAKE THIS TO COURT:

I ask that a heavenly court be convened to hear the evidence in the matter of occult practices in my generations and my own life. I thank You, Lord, that I can enter your court today. I come not in my own righteousness, but in the righteousness of Yeshua, my Lord and Savior. I come under the covering of the word of God and in the blood of Yeshua.

By faith, Lord, I step into your presence and make my petition. Lord, I now ask for a discovery of all my accusers. I ask that they be brought into court bound with chains and fetters of iron according to Psalm 149 and that their lips be mute according to Psalm 31. I acknowledge these accusations as my own sin; I accept responsibility for every time I knowingly and unknowingly participated in occult practices.

I repent for participating in these practices, for believing lies and I receive the blood of Jesus over my spirit, soul and body to dissolve all covenants with evil in me and my generations.

I ask You, Father, to judge me now according to the dispensation of Messiah; I ask You also to judge everything outside of my covering with the same judgment and to judge my accusers with the same judgment.

I ask for restitution and compensation for everything that they have stolen from me and my ancestors and family. I also ask for divorce papers, restraining orders and restraints on the spirits responsible for all of this and I ask that they be kept away from me and my family, loved ones and dear ones.

I receive these papers in my spirit and ask for them to be recorded in my book. By faith, Lord, I ascend into the place of your presence and I step onto the sea of glass. I make an offering of everything I received today and ask that it be recorded in heaven.

I release everything onto the sea of glass just as in Revelation 4:10 the 24 elders cast their crowns before you in an act of worship and honor. I abandon myself to you in holy reverence and awe. I say with those around the throne, "Holy are you, God!"

I give everything to you, Lord, in exchange only for more of you—that out of the realm of heaven I would receive your kingdom. Today, Lord, I go up into my mountain by faith and I take the measure of your kingdom for which I have made a trade and I put it into my mountain in my life and I descend into your presence.

I step out of the place of your presence into this world and I release the mandate from God into this atmosphere and I ask for angelic help in administrating your mandate into the earth in Jesus' name.

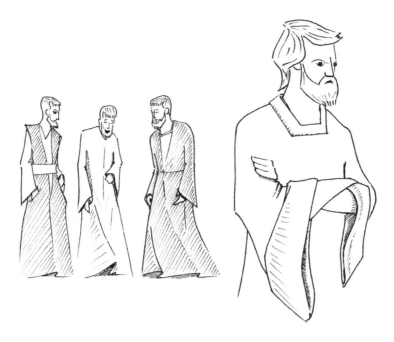

THE STRONGHOLD OF REJECTION

Dana never remembered a time when she felt like she fit in. Her friendships were confusing to her and often ended badly. When she finally married, she secretly felt like her husband chose her because he couldn't find anyone else.

In the early years, she was finishing her graduate thesis and he was teaching at a nearby college. After a long day at work, her husband would come home to their tiny apartment and ask, "How was your day?"

Immediately, Dana would feel defensive. The question she heard was, "What did you do all day—sit at home while I was out working?"

If he asked whether she paid the electric bill, she heard him saying that she wasn't responsible. If the subject of their budget came up, she felt that he didn't love her because he wouldn't care about money if he loved her.

Dana had a stronghold of rejection in her mind. She was sure her thoughts were a true representation of reality but those thoughts were all lies. Her husband loved her and admired her and felt very blessed to have her as his wife.

Other people admired her and often felt insecure in friendships because she had many qualities that intimidated others—an intense sense of purpose, dedication, loyalty and integrity.

She was hard on friends because she was hard on herself and they often disappointed her just as she often was disappointed in herself. She didn't know that perfectionism was preventing her from enjoying relationships.

A stronghold of rejection prevented Dana from seeing her true self with all of the beauty and all of the flaws.

Rejection carries with it a feeling of being unwanted, unaccepted and unloved. You feel like you don't belong, like you are not a member, maybe not even a human being. If you are a woman, you might feel you are not like other women; if you are a man, you might feel like you are not a "real" man.

Rejection cannot receive love or allow you to receive or feel it. You want people to love you desperately, but you are convinced that they don't and you don't deserve to be loved anyway.

Under this stronghold, you are super sensitive to possible signs of rejection and you often question whether people really love you.

Rejection says you are not lovable. If someone is trying to get close to you, rejection will pull away. It may begin treating the other person badly in order to drive them away. Then it says, "See, they didn't really love me."

Rejection comes equipped with a "scrambler" that twists around what people say or do to make it seem like you are being rejected when you aren't. Simple remarks like, "Did you pay the bill?" and "Don't you look good today" become twisted in the way they are heard so that they seem like accusations.

That scrambling is not really coming from you, but from the rejection in you with which you are in agreement.

You find yourself 'walking on eggshells' around a person with rejection. Rejection won't allow you to clarify through honest and open communication what the other person was really intending or meaning to express. Because of fear or hurt, rejection will take you immediately into bitterness. Or it will manifest as rejection of self or of the other person.

Good communication will usually defeat the scrambler or whatever triggers rejection. There may be an honest misunderstanding on your part or an unknowing offense given on theirs.

Strategies for defeating rejection:

1. Recognize it.
2. Take responsibility for agreeing with it.
3. Reject it and choose an alternative explanation.
4. Learn the truth and use the truth to fight the distortions.

Rejection is like propaganda; the same lies told over and over (in your head) seem true. Remember that they are still lies. Most of what we have come to believe as true rejection is only normal human interaction.

God knew you long before He chose to create you. He planned you long before your mother and father were even born. He predestined us to life and redemption before the foundation of the world—we are not accidents or mistakes. We are fully accepted, totally unique, unconditionally loved, forever embraced.

Don't listen to rejection talking to you or casting a shadow on God's feelings for you. You are an awesome work of wonder. Psalm 139:14–15: "I will praise you for I am fearfully and wonderfully made; Marvelous are your works, and that my soul knows very well. My frame was not hidden from you, when I was made in secret, and skillfully wrought in the lowest parts of the earth."

The judgments of the Lord are true and righteous altogether [Psalm 19:9]. Let the Lord decide for you. Were you made to be rejected? Or does He have a better plan?

ASK YOURSELF:

1. How do you think the Lord sees you?

_____

_____

_____

_____

2. How do you see yourself?

_____

_____

_____

_____

3. What would it be like if you stopped believing that you aren't good enough and started believing that you are loved exactly the way you are right now?

_____

_____

_____

_____

Take rejection to court:

Lord, I thank you for your heavenly courts. You are a true and righteous judge. I bring rejection into court and ask for a judgment on this matter. I accept responsibility for agreeing with rejection which is a lie against your very nature. I confess that I have made a covenant with this lie. I accept responsibility for rejection in my bloodline and repent for this sin in my family on both sides going all the way back to the beginning.

Jesus, I thank you for your blood which you gave freely to cover this and all sin. I accept the provision of your mercy covenant and bring all of this under your blood today. Father, judge this sin to death and judge me to life.

I ask for restitution and compensation for everything that was stolen from me and my ancestors and family. I also ask for divorce papers, restraining orders and restraints on the spirits responsible for all of this and I ask that they be kept away from me and my family, loved ones and dear ones.

I receive these papers in my spirit and ask for them to be recorded in my book. By faith, Lord, I ascend into the place of your presence and I step onto the sea of glass. I make an offering of everything I received today and ask that it be recorded in heaven.

I release everything onto the sea of glass just as in Revelation 4:10 the 24 elders cast their crowns before you in an act of worship and honor. I abandon myself to you in holy reverence and awe. I say with those around the throne, "Holy are you, God!"

I give everything to you, Lord, in exchange only for more of you—that out of the realm of heaven I would receive your kingdom. Today, Lord, I go up into my mountain by faith and I take the measure of your kingdom for which I have made a trade and I put it into my mountain in my life and I descend into your presence.

I step out of the place of your presence into this world and I release the mandate from God into this atmosphere and I ask for angelic help in administrating your mandate into the earth in Jesus' name.

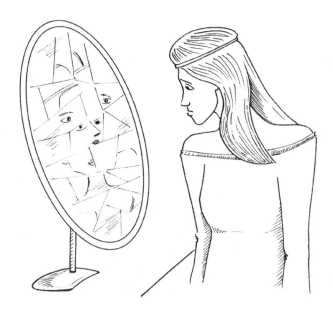

THE STRONGHOLD OF SELF REJECTION

Emily was two different people. On the outside, she was successful, well-liked, a good listener and a loyal friend. Everything she did, she did well. She had a good education, a satisfying job, good friends, a good husband, a nice house and two wonderful children.

Inside, Emily hated herself. Although she acknowledged her blessings in life, she was convinced that (since she didn't deserve them) they would be taken away. She was insecure about her husband's love so she never asked him for anything. She felt unworthy of each of her friends and she was afraid that they would leave her. This led her to become a people pleaser—never saying no to any request no matter how much it might inconvenience her.

She struggled when it came to disciplining the children. They knew that they could get away with anything by saying to their mother,

"I hate you!" Emily could not bear to hear her children verify what she presumed was the truth of their feelings toward her.

Although she seemed quiet and peaceful on the outside, Emily was angry on the inside. She was lonely and afraid. She was sure that no one would ever understand the pain she suffered. She blamed herself but she also blamed God for the years of abuse she had suffered at the hands of her father. Why had God failed to answer her many prayers to be rescued from this hell?

She knew the answer. She wasn't worthy. In her heart of hearts, Emily felt this must be wrong but all the evidence pointed to the same answer. God didn't love her as much as He loved other people or He wouldn't have made her suffer such an awful childhood.

Although she wouldn't admit it, this made Emily angry—really angry. She knew it was no one's fault so she directed her rage where it made the most sense: inward.

Depression was a way of life for her. Sometimes on prescription SSRI's, sometimes off, she attempted suicide; she cut herself; she burned herself with cigarettes. Emily lurched through life hoping and praying for an answer to her agony. Her self-hatred seemed the only thing she could count on.

*　　*　　*

Today, Emily is free of depression and full of joy. She is on a journey of discovery with the Lord. Every day He shows her something new about Himself and something new about herself.

Her restoration is a process.

Here are some things Emily learned about the lies in her head:

The kingdom of self is the inversion of the kingdom of God

It begins with looking inward—often because of abuse or a broken heart. Self-rejection seems normal to you—even virtuous. But when you don't love yourself you are calling God a liar. In the kingdom of self, you are god.

Debasing oneself is pride. Ask yourself if you are listening to God or to your feelings, or to your past, or your circumstances, or your own understanding? Let God be true and all men (and your feelings) be liars.[60]

Choose today to begin living by the truth of who God says you really are in His eyes. Accept yourself unconditionally once and for all and you will defeat self-rejection.

Self-rejection is held in place by self-pity

Self-pity binds you to the past and to pain. It amplifies every thought. It will tell you that you are not loved and that nobody understands you. Self-pity is a total denial that you have a God who actively cares for you. Self-pity says, "What was done to me, I can't get over." It puts your past in charge of your life.[61]

We are saved by God through Christ; we are not to be pitied! We have a God who saves, delivers, prospers, heals, and provides—all according to our real needs and His love and wisdom for us.

---

60 Romans 3:4
61 "For Your Life" Seminar notes, Pastor Henry Wright.

You have to be prepared to take your life back. Fear of self comes from fear of punishment and opens the door to self-hatred. Work to renounce fear so that self-rejection can be dealt with.

Self-pity is the super glue of hell!

Are you harder on yourself than on others? Do you berate yourself? Do you get angry with yourself easily? (Depression counts as self-anger!) Are there things about yourself that you dislike and can't accept? Are there things in your past that you just can't forgive yourself for? How do you talk to yourself when you have done something stupid?

God loves you. He doesn't treat you the way you are treating yourself. It's time to get some truth on the matter of your identity. Follow the voice of God speaking through His Word to you. Inwardly agree with what the Holy Spirit is saying that is true about you and your situation.

Believe it. God really does love you all the time.

Quit listening to the other law—the one in your members.[62] No excuses; no fear. It's time to grow up!

---

62 Romans 7:23

ASK YOURSELF:

1. How do you talk to yourself when you have made a mistake?

_____

_____

_____

_____

2. Are you harder on yourself than others?

_____

_____

_____

_____

3. How does the Father talk to you?

_____

_____

_____

_____

4. Why do you think you are so different from other people?

_____

_____

_____

_____

TAKE SELF-REJECTION TO COURT:

Lord, I thank you for your heavenly courts. You are a true and righteous judge. I bring self-rejection into court and ask for a judgment on this matter. I accept responsibility for agreeing with self-rejection which is a lie against everything you say about my identity. I confess that I have made a covenant with this lie. I accept responsibility for self-rejection in my bloodline and repent for this sin in my family on both sides going all the way back to the beginning.

Jesus, I thank you for your blood which you gave freely to cover this and all sin. I accept the provision of your mercy covenant and bring all of this under your blood today. Father, judge this sin to death and judge me to life.

I ask for restitution and compensation for everything that was stolen from me and my ancestors and family. I also ask for divorce papers, restraining orders and restraints on the spirits responsible for all of this and I ask that they be kept away from me and my family, loved ones and dear ones.

I receive these papers in my spirit and ask for them to be recorded in my book. By faith, Lord, I ascend into the place of your presence and I step onto the sea of glass. I make an offering of everything I received today and ask that it be recorded in heaven.

I release everything onto the sea of glass just as in Revelation 4:10 the 24 elders cast their crowns before you in an act of worship and honor. I abandon myself to you in holy reverence and awe. I say with those around the throne, "Holy are you, God!"

I give everything to you, Lord, in exchange only for more of you—that out of the realm of heaven I would receive your kingdom. Today, Lord, I go up into my mountain by faith and I take the measure of your kingdom for which I have made a trade and I put it into my mountain in my life and I descend into your presence.

I step out of the place of your presence into this world and I release the mandate from God into this atmosphere and I ask for angelic help in administrating your mandate into the earth in Jesus' name.

THE STRONGHOLD OF FEAR

Grace was afraid. The fear had been growing for some time. At first, it was worry—she was worried about school; she was worried about her friends; she was worried about her parents; she was worried about her sisters; she was worried about her own health. What if she died? What if she failed? What if her parents died? What if everything didn't turn out all right?

Worry was a way of life. Her mother was a worrier so this seemed perfectly normal to Grace. She might never have known there was a problem if the worry had stayed manageable. Instead, Grace began to have nightmares and panic attacks.

In her dreams, she was falling or drowning or paralyzed. Every dream made her feel helpless and out of control. She would wake up screaming or crying or sweating.

During the first panic attack, she drove herself to the emergency room. She was sure she was having a heart attack—sure she was going to die. The doctor told her it was 'only' a panic attack; he prescribed anti-anxiety medicine.

Grace was afraid to take the medicine. She read about all of the side effects and decided to take her chances with the panic attacks. As long as she did not do anything to trigger fear, she reasoned that she would not have another attack.

The day Grace had a panic attack in an elevator, she began taking the stairs. The panic attack on an airplane meant she would no longer fly. Soon, wide open spaces caused too much anxiety; roads with more than two lanes became too stressful so she limited her driving to back roads, avoiding all highways.

Before long, Grace began to feel anxiety merely stepping out the front door. At this point, she recognized that fear had taken control of her entire life and now it was threatening to lock her in her house.

*   *   *

It is easy to be sympathetic with Grace. After all, which of us has never worried about anything in our lives? We expect to worry about some things—our kids, money, our health, the future. It is easy to miss the straightforward truth from Scripture that worry is simply a polite word for fear.

Jesus tells his followers not to worry:

> "Then Jesus said to the disciples, 'And so I tell you not to worry about the food you need to stay alive or about the clothes you need for your body. Life is much more important than food, and the body much more important than clothes.

"Look at the crows: they don't plant seeds or gather a harvest; they don't have storage rooms or barns; God feeds them! You are worth so much more than birds! Can any of you live a bit longer by worrying about it? If you can't manage even such a small thing, why worry about the other things?

"Look how the wild flowers grow: they don't work or make clothes for themselves. But I tell you that not even King Solomon with all his wealth had clothes as beautiful as one of these flowers. It is God who clothes the wild grass—grass that is here today and gone tomorrow, burned up in the oven. Won't he be all the more sure to clothe you? What little faith you have!

"So don't be all upset, always concerned about what you will eat and drink. (For the pagans of this world are always concerned about all these things.) Your Father knows that you need these things. 31 Instead, be concerned with his Kingdom, and he will provide you with these things." [Luke 12:22–31]

He makes no distinction between 'worry' and 'fear'.

"Do not be worried and upset," Jesus told them. "Believe in God and believe also in me. There are many rooms in my Father's house, and I am going to prepare a place for you. I would not tell you this if it were not so…Peace is what I leave with you; it is my own peace that I give you. I do not give it as the world does. Do not be worried and upset; do not be afraid." [John 14: 1–3; 27]

Fear is a terrible task master.

WHATEVER IS NOT OF FAITH IS SIN

Fear and faith have one thing in common. They both have a clear expectation of the future.

Romans 14: 23 says that "whatever is not from faith is sin". Since fear is not from faith, fear is sin.

I was teaching this concept recently when a young man in my class began to challenge the idea. We looked at scripture together and agreed that this was the clear teaching of the word but he still felt that this was "harsh".

I asked him a few questions and discovered the problem was his understanding of the concept of sin. Maybe you react to the word "sin" the same way he did. Basically, his idea was that God would judge him for being afraid.

This seemed harsh because he was still operating in a sin-conscious mindset rather than a God-conscious mindset.

2 Corinthians 5:21 says that God made Jesus "become" sin so that we could become "the righteousness of God" in Him. Sin no longer rules over us. We who are in Jesus are the righteousness of God.

When I observe that fear is sin, I am declaring its origin. Fear comes from the sin kingdom. It is an idea whose origin is in darkness. Such things ought not to rule us any longer.

We are in the light.

> "This is the message we have heard from Him and announce to you, that God is Light, and in Him there is no darkness at all. If we say that we have fellowship with Him and yet walk in the darkness, we

lie and do not practice the truth; but if we walk in the Light as He Himself is in the Light, we have fellowship with one another, and the blood of Jesus His Son cleanses us from all sin." [John 1:5–7]

"Let not your heart be troubled, neither let it be afraid."[John 14:27]

The Word of God is Spirit and life to those who find it. Our inner spirit takes life from it. The spirit knows nothing of God except what it receives from hearing the Word of God (seeing God by faith). Without the Word sown in your heart and mind, there is little ability to discern the spirits. Captivity results from a lack of knowledge.

"Therefore my people have **gone into captivity**, because they have no knowledge [Isaiah 5:13]; my people are **destroyed** for lack of knowledge." [Hosea 4:6]

Not every thought you have is your own. Fear can be programmed into a child—especially in the first six years. You may have been taught to be afraid but it wasn't God's idea.

"For God has not given us a spirit of fear, but of power and of love and of a sound mind." [2 Tim 1:7]

If you have fear, your *sound mind* is compromised because fear and anxiety go together. Panic attacks have a spiritual root—psychological stress is by its nature spiritual stress.

Your *love* is compromised because fear causes you to look inward. Self-focus is the opposite of love. Your *power* is compromised because you have no spiritual authority when you are in agreement with a spirit of fear. A house divided against itself will not stand.[63]

---

63 Matthew 12:25; Mark 3:25

Therefore …put off… the old man which grows corrupt according to deceitful lusts, be renewed in the spirit of your mind, and…put on the new man which was created according to God, in true righteousness and holiness [Eph 4:22–24].

FEAR RESULTING FROM TRAUMA

Bad memories can come from trauma, abandonment and abuse and these affect the body. The memories may remain, but the spirit can be cast out. You can have the memory of abuse and no longer have the pain that goes with it.

The pain is caused by the memory combined with the lie that what happened back then is always going to hurt. Break agreement with all lies and establish God's truth over every memory and you will be healed.

2 Corinthians 10:5–6 "…casting down arguments and every high thing that exalts itself against the knowledge of God, *bringing every thought into captivity to the obedience of Christ*, and being ready to punish all disobedience when your obedience is fulfilled."

Your thoughts are not supposed to hold you captive. You are to hold your thoughts captive by carrying them to Christ.

ASK YOURSELF:

1. What is your greatest fear?

    _____

    _____

    _____

    _____

2. Why do you think you are afraid?

    _____

    _____

    _____

    _____

3. What would happen if you chose to trust YHWH in this area?

    _____

    _____

    _____

    _____

4. What are your thoughts on Matthew 6:25: "Therefore I tell you, do not worry about your life, what you will eat or drink; or about your body, what you will wear. Is not life more than food and the body more than clothes?"

    _____

    _____

    _____

    _____

TAKE FEAR TO COURT:

Thank you, Father, for your justice and mercy. You are full of grace and wisdom and I trust you with my past, present, and future. I appeal to the courts of heaven and ask that a hearing begin on the matter of fear.

As I step into your presence, I honor all of those who are here in the court today. I honor the angels who have served and born witness to my life. I honor those in the cloud of witnesses who are here as well as anyone in my bloodline who is here to bear witness to these proceedings. I honor you, Father, Son, and Holy Spirit, three in one, one in three, head of the government of the kingdom of heaven.

I acknowledge now in the presence of all those assembled that I have agreed with a lie. I have opened a door for fear to have access and authority in my life. Today I close that door and seal it with the blood of Jesus. I accept responsibility for agreeing with fear which is a lie against your perfect love. I confess that I have made a covenant with this lie. I accept responsibility for fear in my bloodline and repent for this sin in my family on both sides going all the way back to the beginning.

I repent for every time I agreed with this lie and I receive the blood to answer the sin. I come under the mercy covenant, cover my mind, will and emotions with the blood of Jesus and I ask that you judge everything outside of the blood to death and judge me to life.

Jesus, I thank you for your blood which you gave freely to cover this and all sin. I declare that fear is not from you. You are trustworthy in all things. I will trust you. I accept the provision of your mercy covenant and bring all fear under your blood today. Father, judge this sin to death and judge me to life.

I ask for restitution and compensation for everything that was stolen from me and my ancestors and family because of fear. I take all physical symptoms captive and refuse any agreement with them. I come under your wing into the secret place and abide under your shadow. You are my refuge and strength. I speak truth to my body and I declare all fear and all signs of fear must go in Jesus' name.

I also ask for divorce papers, restraining orders and restraints on the spirits responsible for all of this and I ask that they be kept away from me and my family and my loved ones.

I receive these papers in my spirit and ask for them to be recorded in my book. By faith, Lord, I ascend into the place of your presence and I step onto the sea of glass. I make an offering of everything I received today and ask that it be recorded in heaven.

I release everything onto the sea of glass just as in Revelation 4:10 the twenty-four elders cast their crowns before you in an act of worship and honor. I abandon myself to you in holy reverence and awe. I say with those around the throne, "Holy are you, God!"

I give everything to you, Lord, in exchange only for more of you—that out of the realm of heaven I would receive your kingdom. Today, Lord, I go up into my mountain by faith and I take the measure of your kingdom for which I have made a trade and I put it into my mountain in my life and I descend into your presence.

I step out of the place of your presence into this world and I release the mandate from God into this atmosphere and I ask for angelic help to administrate your mandate into the earth in Jesus' name, Amen.

THE STRONGHOLD OF ENVY & JEALOUSY

Marlene had a difficult life. She was divorced and alone; her only son was killed in a car accident. She had a brother from whom she was estranged and her parents were no longer living. She lived on a small fixed income— enough to get by but she had to live simply.

At church, she made friends with two younger married women. They were not yet retired and so had some disposable income. They were generous and often invited Marlene to share a meal they had cooked. Sometimes they would invite her to lunch and discreetly pick up the check.

Marlene was good company; she was funny, quick witted, and intelligent. She was also proud. Her position as the 'needy one' in her group of friends bothered her greatly. She envied their financial independence, their houses, their families—everything about her two friends caused Marlene to resent them.

She couldn't keep her feelings to herself for long. Just a few months into the friendship, she began to behave badly. She would make comments to belittle one friend to the other.

Each woman became increasingly uncomfortable in Marlene's company. They tried to ignore her behavior. They gave grace in consideration of their friend's difficult situation. They were patient as she became more negative and sarcastic.

Eventually, they chose her company less and less. The friendship grew cold and Marlene was alone again.

*   *   *

Envy will lead you to focus on another person's gifts or possessions or blessings with a covetous heart. This is not only covetousness but idolatry. God will not share us with idols. If we choose to worship other gods, He will release us to our own choice and remove His protection from us.

The scriptures warn us that idolatry is spiritual harlotry and God judges our unfaithfulness. Any person, place or thing that captivates our heart will lead us into agreement with the lie of envy and envy will lead us to the sin of idolatry.

"**Envy** is rottenness of the bones" [Prov. 14:30]

"For anger slays the foolish man, and jealousy kills the simple." [Job 5:2]

"And just as they did not see fit to acknowledge God any longer, God gave them over to a depraved mind, to do those things which are not proper, being filled with all unrighteousness, wickedness, greed, evil; full of **envy**, murder, strife, deceit, malice; they are gossips, slanderers, haters of God, insolent, arrogant, boastful, inventors of evil, disobedient to parents, without understanding, untrustworthy, unloving, unmerciful… [Romans 1:28-31]

And He was saying, "That which proceeds out of the man is what defiles the man. "For from within, out of the heart of men, proceed the evil thoughts, fornications, thefts, murders, adulteries, deeds of **coveting** and wickedness, as well as deceit, sensuality, **envy**, slander, pride, and foolishness. [Mark 7:20-22]

"Who is wise and understanding among you? Let him show by good conduct that his works are done in the meekness of wisdom. But if you have bitter envy and self-seeking in your hearts, do not boast and lie against the truth. This wisdom does not descend from above, but is earthly, sensual, and demonic.

For where envy and self-seeking exist, confusion and every evil thing are there. But the wisdom that is from above is first pure, then peaceable, gentle, willing to yield, full of mercy and good fruits, without partiality and without hypocrisy. Now the fruit of righteousness is sown in peace by those who make peace." [James 3:13ff]

Now the deeds of the flesh are evident: immorality, impurity, sensuality, idolatry, sorcery, enmities, strife, jealousy, out bursts of anger, disputes, dissensions, factions, **envying**, drunkenness, carousing, and things like these, of which I forewarn you, just as I have forewarned you, that those who practice such things will not inherit the kingdom of God. [Galatians 5:19-21]

What is the difference between envy and jealousy?

Envy is a feeling of discontent or competition when considering the blessings others possess. It is often accompanied by covetousness which is longing for someone else's possessions, talents or blessings. Envy fosters greed.

Jealousy is guarding something you already have, refusing to share and treating the blessings of God as your undisputed personal possessions.

In relationships, jealousy causes possessiveness, suspicion and distrust of your partner. It even creates a climate of abuse in which friends are seen as rivals to be eliminated. Jealousy destroys relationships, families and marriages.

It is the nature of envy and jealousy to lead you to compare yourself to other people. Envy and jealousy will lead you into division. It can even keep you out of the Body of Christ. Other people's envy can steal your joy.

The roots of envy and jealousy

Envy and jealousy are rooted in pride and bitterness. The elder brother in the parable of the prodigal son provides a good example of envy and jealousy. His pride in the work he did for his father and in his faithfulness compared to his brother's foolishness drove him to bitterness.

While their father was praying and watching for his son's return, this brother simmered in envy and jealousy, comparing himself favorably to his reckless sibling. Envy and jealousy whispered into his ear, drawing his eyes to himself and to his brother rather than to his father and to the blessings he enjoyed every day.

Weren't his blessings always there? There is no indication in the story that his father withheld anything from him. When his brother returned, his father said to him, "Son, you have always been with me, and all that is mine is yours."

The older son could not understand his father's heart. He missed the opportunity for grace. He imagined that his father was guilty of showing favoritism all because he measured goodness based on his own behavior. This is pride.

It's easy for us to think we wouldn't react that way but we should think again. Have you ever committed adultery? If not, it would be easy to feel superior to someone who has. How about something less flagrant?

Have you ever compared your attendance to church services with that of others? Or what about thinking that you volunteer for more service or that you give more than others?

These are examples of self righteousness and if we focus on our own righteousness comparing our performance to others' we will find ourselves wide open to the stronghold of envy and jealousy.

Envy and jealousy causes us to begrudge the grace God shows those who we feel undeserving. When we respond to someone's testimony with envy, it causes dissonance in the spiritual realm and evil works are released.

The presence of envy and jealousy is evidence that inferiority and insecurity is at work in our thinking. Are you distracted by thoughts like, "Why is he/she getting blessed right now when I have been working so hard to be faithful? I don't see the same blessings in my life. It doesn't seem fair!"

When we are looking at each other and comparing ourselves to one another, we have changed our focus. This is the goal of our enemy. If we continually focus on each other, we will miss out on the plan and purpose of Heaven.

Keep your eyes on Jesus! What is He saying? What is He doing? Remember that Jesus is our model[64] and He only did what He saw His Father doing.[65] This is our standard!

---

64 1 John 4:17
65 John 5:19

ASK YOURSELF:

1. How often do you compare yourself to others?

   _____
   _____
   _____
   _____

2. Do you have a preoccupation with fairness?

   _____
   _____
   _____
   _____

3. When others are praised, promoted or blessed, do you have a hard time being genuinely happy for them?

   _____
   _____
   _____
   _____

4. Describe a time when you thought you were treated unfairly.

   _____
   _____
   _____
   _____

TAKE ENVY AND JEALOUSY TO COURT:

Lord, I thank you for your heavenly courts. You are a true and righteous judge. I bring envy and jealousy into court and ask for a judgment on this matter. I accept responsibility for agreeing with envy and jealousy which is a lie against your wisdom and love. I confess that I have made a covenant with this lie. I accept responsibility for envy and jealousy in my bloodline and repent for this sin in my family on both sides going all the way back to the beginning.

Jesus, I thank you for your blood which you gave freely to cover this and all sin. I declare that envy and jealousy is not from you. You are trustworthy in all things. I will trust you. I accept the provision of your mercy covenant and bring all envy and jealousy under your blood today. Father, judge this sin to death and judge me to life.

I ask for restitution and compensation for everything that was stolen from me and my ancestors and family because of envy and jealousy. I take all physical symptoms captive and refuse any agreement with them. I come under your wing into the secret place and abide under your shadow.

You are my refuge and strength. I speak truth to my body and I declare all envy and jealousy and all physical consequences of envy and jealousy must go in Jesus' name.

I also ask for divorce papers, restraining orders and restraints on the spirits responsible for any further temptation or torment and I ask that they be kept away from me and my family and my loved ones.

I receive these papers in my spirit and ask for them to be recorded in my book. By faith, Lord, I ascend into the place of your presence and I step onto the sea of glass. I make an offering of everything I received today and ask that it be recorded in heaven.

I release everything onto the sea of glass just as in Revelation 4:10 the 24 elders cast their crowns before you in an act of worship and honor. I abandon myself to you in holy reverence and awe. I say with those around the throne, "Holy are you, God!"

I give everything to you, Lord, in exchange only for more of you—that out of the realm of heaven I would receive your kingdom. Today, Lord, I go up into my mountain by faith and I take the measure of your kingdom for which I have made a trade and I put it into my mountain in my life and I descend into your presence.

I step out of the place of your presence into this world and I release the mandate from God into this atmosphere and I ask for angelic help in administrating your mandate into the earth in Jesus' name, amen.

THE STRONGHOLD OF ADDICTION

Dan came from a good family. His parents loved each other and
his brothers and sisters were close. Cigarettes and alcohol came
into his life at a young age. Before long, he was smoking marijuana;
after that, he experimented with cocaine, various pills, heroin, and
finally crystal meth.

No one else in Dan's family used drugs but his brother was an
alcoholic and one sister was a shopaholic. His mother had difficulty
with her weight because she used food for comfort. His father was
a workaholic.

Everyone in the family struggled with the stronghold of addiction
but only Dan chose illegal drugs and only Dan went to prison. It was
difficult for Dan's family; they had never known anyone who went
to prison. They loved Dan but they were ashamed. It took them a
long time to come to terms with Dan's choices.

Dan went into treatment and stopped using drugs. He is clean and sober and out of prison but the members of his family still struggle with addiction. Because they chose legal, acceptable ways to feed their addiction, each of them found a way to rationalize their behavior by comparing it favorably with Dan's. The choice to use drugs almost ruined Dan's life but it also saved him. He had no choice but to deal with his addiction—he had hit bottom.

Addictions of every kind are on the rise in our culture today. In the scriptures, the word 'addiction' is not found. The closest concept is 'besetting sins.'

There are two important principles to remember in the fight for victory over this stronghold. First, it takes **surrender** to God to get free of an addiction and second, addictions are powerful because of their spiritual component.

> "Then God spoke all these words, saying, "I am the Lord your God, who brought you out of the land of Egypt, out of the house of slavery. You shall have no other gods before Me. **You shall not make for yourself an idol, or any likeness of what is in heaven above or on the earth beneath or in the water under the earth. You shall not worship them or serve them**; for I, the Lord your God, am a jealous God, visiting the iniquity of the fathers on the children, on the third and the fourth generations of those who hate Me but showing loving-kindness to thousands, to those who love Me and keep My commandments." [Exodus 20:1–7]

Anyone who has been addicted knows the power of the substance or the behavior to which he/she is addicted. The spiritual component becomes obvious when we try to break free. It is an addiction when there is a forceful pull on our time, attention, and resources. That force is spiritual.

The physical component of addiction to any chemical substance is well known. Once the substance is introduced to the body, the body begins to crave it as a physiological response and any attempt to suspend use of the substance can produce physical symptoms known as 'withdrawal'.

Behavioral addictions like shopping, talking, attention seeking, high-risk behaviors, sexual addiction, etc. have a chemical component as well which is tied to body chemistry. The release of dopamine or adrenaline can create a physiological reward system which creates a craving for more.

Victory over any addiction, over anything that holds you in bondage, never comes through will-power. It is not a matter of being good enough, or strong enough, or perfect enough.

Victory comes through a truth encounter. You do not have the power to defeat your enemies; God does. The truth is what unites you by faith to God's power. *"If you continue in my word you shall be my disciples indeed and you shall know the truth and the truth will make you free."* [66]

So what is the truth? There are three main truths behind addiction which must be reckoned with. First, addictive substances and behaviors carry a voice that invites you into rest. You are agitated and uncomfortable (either consciously or unconsciously) and the thought comes to mind that you should eat or drink or take or do something in order to feel better. This is the voice of an idol saying, "Come to me and I will give you rest." It is a false promise, of course. There is no rest in addiction; there is bondage and death. The proper response—the one that earns you your freedom—is to step into your identity and shut the voice down.

---

66 John 8:32

Repent of ever believing the lie and turn toward your heavenly Father.

The second truth we must see about addiction is that we often have a fundamentally flawed view of our heavenly Father. This often comes from a broken relationship with our earthly father. We call this a "father wound" and it will distort your image of our loving, kind, approachable Abba who longs to bring you close to Himself.

If we find ourselves unable to accept the love of Yahweh, a father wound is likely the cause. We must let Him heal our heart. Repentance will involve turning toward Him and learning to trust His love. No matter what our wounds tell us, we must trust Him in order to be healed.

The third truth we must face is that our wounded hearts[67] can become the object of our attention to the point that we are unable to accept any responsibility for our own healing. We cannot be content to remain victims whose identity is found in our suffering and loss. WE MUST REJECT SELF-PITY!!

Self-pity is the voice that focuses on your circumstances instead of the Lord. It is the voice that is telling you what you "need" and what you "deserve". Self-pity is the voice of compromise when faced with a challenge. It is the voice that urges you to say, "This is good enough" instead of, "Have you yet shed blood in the resisting of sin?" [Heb. 12:4] Self-pity is the voice that says, "No one is perfect so how can you expect so much of yourself?"

It uses just enough truth to seem reasonable but it is a false spirit that puts your comfort over holiness. Self-pity is the devil's voice.

---

67 The idea of three lies supporting addiction is attributed to Rev. Steve Evans. I am not aware of a published work on the subject but I have heard Rev. Evans teach this on many occassions.

It is the super glue of hell and every damned thing from the pit of hell sticks to it. If you look underneath rejection, rebellion, fear, anger, addiction, depression, accusation, and every other stronghold, you will find some form of self-pity—some rationalization that is telling you to accept the lie and sleep with the enemy.

If we continually turn inward to our woundedness we will become helpless babies always asking others to pray for us or minister to us but never walking any of our healing into maturity. Suffering can make you a deeply compassionate person or it can turn you into a bitter, self-absorbed husk. It's your choice.

Repentance will require you to turn away from self-worship and turn towards your heavenly Father. You will find everything you need in Him.

ASK YOURSELF:

1. List the substances or activities that bring you comfort or help with your emotions, attitude or energy.

   _____

   _____

   _____

   _____

2. Have any of these become something you can no longer stop doing?

   _____

   _____

   _____

   _____

3. Describe what you are doing to address the need for healing in your heart.

   _____

   _____

   _____

   _____

TAKE ADDICTION TO COURT:

Lord, I thank you for your heavenly courts. You are a true and righteous judge. I bring addiction into court and ask for a judgment on this matter. I accept responsibility for agreeing with addiction which is idolatry. I confess that I have made a covenant with this lie. I accept responsibility for addiction in my bloodline and repent for this sin in my family on both sides going all the way back to the beginning.

Jesus, I thank you for your blood which you gave freely to cover this and all sin. I accept the provision of your mercy covenant and bring all of this under your blood today. Father, judge this sin to death and judge me to life.

I ask for restitution and compensation for everything that was stolen from me and my ancestors and family. I also ask for divorce papers, restraining orders and restraints on the spirits responsible for all of this and I ask that they be kept away from me and my family, loved ones and dear ones.

I receive these papers in my spirit and ask for them to be recorded in my book. By faith, Lord, I ascend into the place of your presence and I step onto the sea of glass. I make an offering of everything I received today and ask that it be recorded in heaven.

I release everything onto the sea of glass just as in Revelation 4:10 the twenty-four elders cast their crowns before you in an act of worship and honor. I abandon myself to you in holy reverence and awe. I say with those around the throne, "Holy are you, God!"

I give everything to you, Lord, in exchange only for more of you—that out of the realm of heaven I would receive your kingdom. Today, Lord, I go up into my mountain by faith and I take the measure of your kingdom for which I have made a trade and I put it into my mountain in my life and I descend into your presence.

I step out of the place of your presence into this world and I release the mandate from God into this atmosphere and I ask for angelic help in administrating your mandate into the earth in Jesus' name.

3. GOING FORWARD

AN OVERCOMER'S DECLARATION

WALKING IT OUT

AN OVERCOMER'S DECLARATION

This is an example of how to apply the principles of this book when you have been wronged. I wrote this to a friend and prayer partner about five years ago after a particularly painful experience with rejection and accusation. Words were said; unjust accusations were leveled against me by someone very close to me.

The fight to bring my pain under the cross and the blood was significant. With the grace of God and the help of my praying friend, I broke through before the sun had set. In the hope that this declaration might help you in your battle to overcome, I include it in this book.

So here is how I see the events of today after a shower, a rest and an hour of reading the word:

I can either curl up in a ball with my hurt feelings or I can come out of this attack fighting. I choose to fight. I refuse to let the enemy steal my promises. I will not let any demon from hell tell me lies about my past, present or future. I will not allow the kingdom of darkness to rule my thinking to draw me into hopelessness or victim thinking or self-pity.

I am a warrior. I was made for the fight. My promises are MINE and no one can take them away! I will NOT surrender my future. I will NOT surrender my hope. Nothing passes into or out of my life without the Lord's permission. If He allows it, it is for my good and for the good of everyone around me.

Rejection is a lie. I am accepted in the Beloved. Rude behavior on the part of others is simply a failure of love. I must pray for them more. I choose to forgive. I will not be destroyed by the words of another human being. I will not accept anything into my heart without passing it through the fire of love first. My love is His love and His love is an all consuming fire. Everything—absolutely everything—must yield to the cross of my Beloved as it burns in my heart.

When I prayed, "More of you, Jesus," this is what it looks like: More opportunities to love when I am being injured; more chances to forgive when I am wounded; more of the cross over my emotions. He knows me. He loves me. That is enough.

Thank you for your tireless intercession today. I think I am going to be alright. :)

That's it! Every attack of the enemy is an opportunity to choose. Take it to court; repent and accept responsibility; forgive everyone involved and ask for the matter to be judged through the mercy covenant. Go to the throne of God's justice to deal with the sin that is afflicting you. You have standing in the courts of heaven! Always come under the blood covenant of Jesus—the mercy covenant—and ask to be judged through the covenant (never on your own merits).

Realize that the fight to overcome is a fight to humble yourself!

[James 4:10]

WALKING IT OUT

The way forward will require perseverance and patience. We don't change our thinking overnight. It will help to have a friend or two committed to walking out of stronghold thinking with you. When I first began to walk it out, I had a small group of two or three others who also wanted freedom. We met weekly like an AA group. Our rules were simple: listen to each other, listen to ourselves, and listen to Jesus.

Everyone had permission to point out lies that were creeping back into our thinking. We held each other accountable but did it with love and humility, always making ourselves available for correction. No one was in charge; we accepted the responsibility to run the group as equal members.

Our shared goal was intimacy with Jesus. Every toxic way of thinking that interfered with that goal had to go. As we got freer and freer, we became more joyful and more peaceful; our trust in the Lord grew and we began to see the world differently. It became easier to love people.

The numbers in our group have changed and the members have come and gone. I have remained committed to providing a way for people to walk in freedom for more than ten years now. I have seen many changed lives and many miracles. We are still in process, but we are forever changed. The people that knew us before and know us now see the change.

If you want to grow in your relationship with Jesus, to become secure in Him, to trust Him more, you can take the same journey we have taken. You can have a spiritual breakthrough!

FURTHER READING ON LIFE IN THE KINGDOM:

Beyond Human, Justin Abraham

Interior Castle, Teresa of Avila

Pagan Christianity, Frank Viola and George Barna

The Mystic Awakening, Adrian Beale

Behold I Give You Power, Paul E. Billheimer

Realms of the Kingdom, Ian Clayton

You Set My Spirit Free, John of the Cross

Holiness, Truth, and the Presence of God, Francis Frangipane

Living a Supernatural Life, James W. Goll

Supernatural, Michael S. Heiser

Operating in the Courts of Heaven, Robert Henderson

There Were Two Trees In The Garden, Rick Joyner

The God Who is there, Francis Schaeffer

ABOUT THE AUTHOR

Elizabeth Ruggles Woods has served in leadership and teaching roles for more than 35 years, as worship leader, Bible study teacher, adult Sunday school teacher, children's ministry coordinator, conference speaker and coordinator, and most recently in prophetic intercession, teaching and training the body of Christ to walk in freedom.

Beth is a wife of 34 years and the mother of two grown boys. She holds undergraduate degrees in Religion, Philosophy and Psychology; advanced degrees in International Development Sociology, Education and Counseling. She has been used by God in an amazing variety of ways from college classrooms to children's ministry; as a missionary to street kids in New York City and to village churches in Tanzania.

She has been a leader in an organic church for more than ten years and is currently an itinerate teacher to a group of nonprofit discipleship training centers throughout the U.S.

A counselor and teacher by profession, Beth has a heart for those who are hurting and a passion to see the body of Christ set free from all that hinders us in our high calling.

Rev 19:6-8

Made in the USA
Middletown, DE
10 January 2019